GLOBALIZATION AND INSTITUTIONAL ADJUSTMENT

In memory of my father,
Prof. Dr. Friedrich Hülsemeyer.

He left too early for his copy of this book.

Globalization and Institutional Adjustment

Federalism as an Obstacle?

AXEL HÜLSEMEYER
Department of Political Science,
Concordia University,
Montreal, Canada

Routledge
Taylor & Francis Group
LONDON AND NEW YORK

First published 2004 by Ashgate Publishing

Reissued 2018 by Routledge
2 Park Square, Milton Park, Abingdon, Oxon OX14 4RN
711 Third Avenue, New York, NY 10017, USA

Routledge is an imprint of the Taylor & Francis Group, an informa business

Typeset by IML Typographers, Birkenhead, Merseyside

A Library of Congress record exists under LC control number: 2004007705

ISBN 13: 978-0-815-38926-2 (hbk)
ISBN 13: 978-1-351-15728-5 (ebk)

Contents

List of Figures and Tables

Figures

Table

Preface

The origins of this book go back to my time as a graduate student. While still in Germany, I studied both the significant deepening of European economic integration since the mid-1980s, as well as its restrictive implications for the policymaking capacity of the Länder, that is, the component governments of the then still only federal member state of the European Community.

After I had moved to Canada, I became acutely aware of the differences that the far more limited North American economic integration nonetheless had on Canadian federalism, and this primarily because of the latter's distinct political institutions. In my doctoral work at the University of Calgary, I set out to explore the extent to which economic globalization constraints affected, if at all, the ability of states to adjust their political institutions to this process. Can variation be discerned across different liberal democratic political systems? Are some of them more conducive to capturing and regulating the increased market size, which itself is viewed as a consequence of a globalized economy?

In this vein, this book examines how constitutional provisions influence the way in which countries adapt to the process of economic globalization. More specifically, the study attempts to systematically investigate the causal relationship between regional integration and federal countries through the theoretical and analytical apparatus of International Political Economy. It is claimed in the literature that states must continuously adjust their institutions to this phenomenon by shifting the provision of certain public goods to different governmental levels. Against this backdrop, the study generates three hypotheses based on the economic sub-discipline of Fiscal Federalism to determine the precise conditions under which a reassignment of domestic public sector functions at a supranational level in view of global economic pressures would be welfare-optimal. However, since these *outcome*-oriented propositions cannot account for the considerable variation that exists in the ratification and/or implementation of PTAs, I draw on literature that emphasizes the mediating role of extant domestic institutions.

The conclusion of preferential trade agreements (PTAs) is seen as the most visible 'state' response in this context, albeit with varying degrees of institutionalization. These regional integration schemes are based on international treaties that subsequently must be ratified and implemented by the signatory states. While this poses no difficulty for unitary countries, it can become problematic in federations if, as is increasingly the case, provisions in these economic agreements encroach upon powers that domestically fall under subnational jurisdiction. Would federalism *in general* then have to be considered an obstacle?

Contrary to some of the literature, the study suggests that, analogous to the general juxtaposition of unitary and federal states, there are marked differences *among* federations in both the speed and manner of political-institutional adjustment, which depend on the *degree* of centralization. Here I will utilize, but modify, the concept of institutional veto players, the principle tenet of which is that the more decentralized a political system is, the more difficult it becomes to instigate political change (that is, the domestic ratification and implementation of an international economic treaty). To examine this proposition, the investigation traces the institutional adjustment to PTAs in the 1980s and 1990s in Germany and Canada, as these two countries are viewed as the centralized and decentralized poles, respectively, on a continuum of OECD federations. The empirical analysis covers the ratification of the Single European Act and the Maastricht Treaty in Germany and then contrasts it with the implementation of the bilateral CUSFTA and the NAFTA, including the latter's side agreements, in Canada. The conclusion briefly discusses the role of the respective component governments in the Uruguay Round of the GATT, that is, an instance where both countries ultimately signed the *same* treaty.

A number of people have made significant contributions to bringing this project to completion, albeit often unknowingly so. First, at the University of Calgary, I am grateful for the academic advice that Jim Keeley, Roger Gibbins and Stan Drabek have provided, as well as the untiring support of Ella Wensel and Judi Powell in all administrative and personal matters. Second, I am indebted to Pat James at the University of Missouri-Columbia who has become a most appreciated mentor and friend. Third, at Concordia University, I wish to thank my colleagues in the Department of Political Science, and particularly the caring concern of Reeta Tremblay, for the friendly and productive atmosphere in which I was able to finalize the manuscript. Fourth, the ideational and financial support of my parents has been unwavering; this is of special significance to me, as they have allowed their only child to embark on an academic career half a world away. Finally, one's partner invariably bears the heaviest load, tolerating and learning to live with the frustrations that at certain stages accompany academic work. Over the years, Sarah Tarry helped me with her love and constructive criticism, always keeping the spirit up with her positive personality. She is my biggest source of strength.

List of Abbreviations

APC	Annual Premiers' Conference
BL	Basic Law (German constitution)
CA	Constitution Act (Canada)
CCTN	Continuing Committee on Trade Negotiations
CFSP	Common Foreign and Security Policy (one of the three pillars of the Maastricht Treaty)
CIA	Canadian Intergovernmental Agreement
CMTN	Committee on Multilateral Trade Negotiations
CUSFTA	Canada-United States Free Trade Agreement
C-NAFTA	Committee on NAFTA Negotiations
EC	European Community (until the Maastricht Treaty)
ECJ	European Court of Justice
ECU	European Currency Unit (the predecessor of the single currency)
ERDF	European Reconstruction and Development Fund
ERT	European Roundtable of Industrialists
EU	European Union (since the Maastricht Treaty)
FDI	Foreign Direct Investment
FMC	First Ministers' Conference
FRG	Federal Republic of Germany (West Germany, 1949-90; Germany since 1990)
FTAA	Free Trade Agreement of the Americas
FTC	Free Trade Commission
GATT	General Agreement on Tariffs and Trade
GDP	Gross Domestic Product
GDR	German Democratic Republic (East Germany, 1949-90)
IPE	International Political Economy (as an academic discipline)
JHA	Justice and Home Affairs (one of the three pillars of the Maastricht Treaty)
MNC	Multinational Corporation
NAAEC	North American Agreement on Environmental Cooperation
NAALC	North American Agreement on Labor Cooperation
NAFTA	North American Free Trade Agreement
NTB	Non-tariff Barrier
OECD	Organization for Economic Cooperation and Development
POGG	Peace, Order, and Good Government (national legislative principle in the Canadian Constitution [sec. 91])
PSF	Public Sector Function

PTA	Preferential Trade Agreement (economic regionalism)
QMV	Qualified Majority Voting
SEA	Single European Act
TEU	Treaty on European Union (the so-called Maastricht Treaty)
VP	Veto Player
WEU	Western European Union (the defense arm of the EU)
WTO	World Trade Organization

Chapter 1

Introduction: Globalization, 'the State' and 'the Market'

> Once again, it must be emphasized that the unity which giant capitalism postulates in the economic sphere postulates a corresponding unity in the conference of political powers upon the federal government.
> Harold J. Laski (1939), 'The obsolescence of federalism', *The New Republic: A Journal of Opinion*, 3 May: 369.

The discipline of International Political Economy (IPE) is at its core concerned with the relationship between the two dominant forms of social organization in the modern world, 'the state' and 'the market'. It is the role of the state to regulate the market and to provide public goods that the market would not otherwise produce in sufficient quantities. Scholars and the general public alike may have different, ideologically motivated, views on the *degree* to which this should be the case, but the state's general function in the economy is beyond doubt.

The argument advanced in the epigraph, by contrast, is that a specific state *form* was increasingly unsuited to fulfil this function. Laski maintained, with a particular view to the American political system, that 'giant capitalism', as he called it, demanded an organization of political authority that would effectively match it in size. Hence, 'the state' required a higher degree of centralization, so as to avoid domestic fragmentation between different levels of government that could be played off against each other by what we would now call multinational corporations (MNCs). Laski went even further and famously suggested that, in general, 'the epoch of federalism is over' (1939: 367).

About half a century later, two sets of reactions to his comments can be discerned. First, the principle tenets of his argumentation reappear in the debate about the impact of 'globalization' for the future of 'the state' (among others, Cerny, 1995; Hirst and Thompson, 1995; Evans, 1997). Second, those sympathetic to the federal cause, especially in its most decentralized version, point out that Laski's prediction obviously turned out to be premature, since federalism has not disappeared but, on the contrary, according to their view is rather successfully established (Bakvis and Chandler, 1987a). I will briefly discuss these two assessments in turn, for the present study is based on the link between them.

Pendulum Swings: Globalization and Economic Regionalism

The concept of 'globalization' has quickly become a popular catchphrase in contemporary social science, and the academic debate on the phenomenon seems extensive;[1] yet, notions still range from the withering away of the state (Ohmae, 1995) to an actual increase in its policy-making capacity (Hirst and Tompson, 1995; Evans, 1997).[2] I suggest that we can organize the debate within IPE as being conducted from either a more structural or a rather actor-centered perspective, although these are not mutually exclusive. In the structural view, 'internationalization' (Milner and Keohane, 1996),[3] is conceptualized as the 'exogenous easing of international exchange' (Frieden and Rogowski, 1996). This means that the well-known advances in communications and transportation technology increase the number of internationally tradable goods and services versus non-tradable ones and subsequently result in relative price changes. *Internationally*, while state and market geographically coincided from the industrial revolution onward, the process of (economic) globalization, it is charged, is increasingly challenging this connection. In an age of global finance and multinational corporations, states can no longer capture the market that they wish to regulate; the latter has outgrown the former in size, and we can think of this as a pendulum swing toward 'the market'.

There are principally two ways in which 'the state' can, and does, react to the now increased range of large economic actors beyond its immediate reach. Empirically, they almost always occur in tandem, but the literature discusses them separately, depending on the scholarly focus. First, Cerny (1995) asserts that globalization forces state governments to continually adjust their political institutions to this process. In his terminology, the 'optimal political economies of scale' are changing,[4] leading to a shift from the welfare state to what he terms the 'competition state'. The latter necessitates a new role for policy makers as primarily being brokers and active promoters of the economic attractiveness of their constituencies for MNCs and foreign investors. Cerny sees this development as practically *inevitable*, regardless of whether or not one considers it desirable; hence, this structural viewpoint exhibits a form of technological determinism. It is also merely a *domestic* 'solution'; endeavoring to entice FDI does, by definition, not address the spatial mismatch between 'state' and 'market', that is, the ability of the former to *regulate* the latter. To do so calls for enlarging the size of political authority through the pooling of certain state responsibilities in the economy.

Thus, the conclusion of, economically motivated, macro-regional integration schemes is the second option for the 'state' to tackle the increased 'market' size emanating from the process of economic globalization. The empirical proliferation of 'preferential trade agreements' (PTAs), which has taken place since the mid-1980s, has sparked considerable scholarly attention (Mansfield and Milner, 1999). While many studies remain focused on European and North American schemes, more emphasis has also recently been given to Latin America, Asia-Pacific and even the Middle East (among others, Bowles and MacLean, 1996; Jenkins, 1999; Lawson, 1999). There appears to be a general agreement that the accelerated pace of integration in the last two decades is usefully understood as a political-institutional *response* to the process of economic globalization (Gress, 1996; Coleman and Underhill, 1998), for nation-states find it increasingly difficult to continually provide certain public goods by themselves. Put differently, PTAs are an attempt to swing the pendulum back toward 'the state'.[5]

Public Sector Shifts: Fiscal Federalism

With this new role of the state, Cerny maintains it has become too big for the provision of certain public goods (for example technical infrastructure), which may be devolved to a subnational level. Conversely, the state has become too small for a variety of other public goods that are suited to be supranationalized (for instance environmental protection); some might remain on the national level (say, defense), while a few could be organized through self-regulation of the market (among them the banking sector). This begs the question about the *conditions* under which we can expect the movement of *which kinds* of public goods to *which* governmental level.[6] Cerny developed a number of hypotheses based on his argument about *who* is likely to provide different public goods in the future (1995: 621–5); yet, these propositions are left so ambiguous as to be virtually untestable.[7]

I suggest that we can draw on the economic sub-discipline of Fiscal Federalism to develop clearer propositions about the circumstances under which the shift of certain kinds of public sector functions (PSFs) is more likely to occur. Fiscal Federalism is concerned with the welfare-optimal assignment of PSFs among various levels of government. 'Optimal' means the *simultaneous* achievement of an efficient allocation of resources and an equitable distribution of income (Oates, 1972). The former concept lends itself well to economic analysis, whereas the latter depends upon the consensus in a given society about what constitutes 'equity'. The three PSFs that Fiscal Federalism conceptualizes are the stabilization (that is, monetary and fiscal policies), redistribution (the conventional understanding of the welfare state) and allocation functions (namely market regulations and the provision of public goods). As I will argue in Chapter 2, an extrapolation of fiscal federalist logic beyond the national realm for which it was conceived would precisely propose the *supranationalization* of most of these PSFs, albeit to different degrees (Hülsemeyer, 2000).[8] This holds under the premise that the economic interdependence *among* the member states of a macro-region clearly outweighs the trading links with any other country or region.[9]

Two limitations exist with Fiscal Federalism: first, its propositions are *normative* in the sense that they prescribe what governments *should* do. Whether or not this is indeed what they are doing is an empirical question.

Second, the discipline draws a *direct* causal link from a change in the economic environment (here: globalization) to the 'appropriate' government response (here: the signing of a macro-regional treaty). Thus, it remains unclear from its hypotheses *why* they hold or not, and *where* along the way, if so, a proposition failed.

Analytically, these aspects can be addressed through a comparative case study that traces the institutional adaptation to economic globalization in different countries. This brings us to the more actor-centered view of the globalization debate.[10]

Constitutions and Veto Players

Economic globalization leads to relative price changes for groups of producers and consumers, in turn prompting alterations in the preferences of *domestic* economic and political actors about state policies and institutions, as well as the relative power of those preferences.[11] As the number of actors expecting to benefit from global competition increases, they will favor and push for deregulation, privatization and a curbing of Keynesian policies. When their influence relative to those wishing to maintain a level of protection increases, policy makers are likely to adhere to these new demands (Frieden and Rogowski, 1996). However, while the preferences of domestic actors are undoubtedly relevant, they frequently do *not* directly translate into policy changes, for these preferences are constrained through extant domestic institutions. The latter mediate between altered demands by economic and societal actors as a result of exogenous economic change (that is, globalization); they include, for instance, the distinction between pluralist and neo-corporatist organizations of the labor market, but also, and more importantly, 'formal public institutions' (Garrett and Lange, 1996). Most pervasive among the latter in their impact on policymaking are constitutional frameworks because they are most resistant to change.

The general proposition is that the more centralized a political system is, the easier a policy change can be instituted, that is, the less resistance has to be overcome by those actors wishing to alter the *status quo*. This argument is based on the veto player (VP) theory developed by Tsebelis (1995); an institutional VP has the constitutionally entrenched power to ultimately block a government decision, regardless of whether or not this ability is exercised in a particular situation. The VP concept works on the premise that political actors legitimized by differently sized constituencies will exhibit distinct interests in their dealings with each other; for instance, federal and provincial governments in Canada have national and subnational constituencies, respectively, and *therefore* will have different positions. Institutional VPs are a particular feature of bicameralism – in contrast to partisan VPs that exist in all (at least liberal democratic) political systems. By definition, federalism always has two chambers;[12] since the *number* of VPs matters, the more decentralized a federation is, the more institutional problems its national government is expected to have in pushing through a policy change.[13]

Regional Integration and Federalism

Macro-regional (economic) integration schemes are based on international trade treaties that require subsequent ratification and implementation in the signatory countries before they can come into force; this is not contentious in unitary states, as the provision of *all* PSFs by definition is a national competence. It *can*, however, become a problem in federations, namely if the treaty under consideration covers topics that domestically do not fall under exclusive federal but at least in part also subnational jurisdiction (Richards, 1991). Precisely this is increasingly the case since the mid-1980s with trade agreements at both the macro-regional and global levels. In Europe, the Single European Act of 1986, establishing the common market, and even more so the Maastricht Treaty, left virtually no subnational competence of the only established federal member state at the time, Germany, untouched.[14] In North America, particularly the NAFTA and its side agreements on labor and the environment touched on areas firmly under the jurisdiction of the Canadian provinces. Finally, with the so-called Uruguay Round under the auspices of the General Agreement on Tariffs and Trade (GATT), the highly contentious subjects of agriculture and government procurement entered multilateral trade negotiations for the first time. Again, these are areas that in *some* federations in part depend on the competencies of the component governments.

Laski Revisited

The Federalist Answer

The potential implications of the institutional VP argument to which the IPE literature (among others, Garrett and Lange, 1996) refers are twofold: first, federal systems *at large* may be an obstacle to policy change relative to unitary states. Second, *among* federations, the resistance to institutional adjustment should increase with the degree of decentralization. It should therefore not come as a surprise that the academic response to this assessment, which largely mirrors Laski's proposition, has been articulated almost exclusively by those sympathetic to the cause of federalism in its decentralized form.[15]

On the first account, it was formulated as a major research question within the federalist literature whether unitary or federal systems are more flexible in their adjustment to economic globalization (Boeckelman, 1996).[16] Gibbins (1987) suggests that, given the 'stickiness' of federal constitutions, the adjustment might follow a rather incremental and informal manner compared to what is possible in a unitary system. Brown and Smith (1991) edited a volume that examined whether the comparatively extremely decentralized constitutional separation of powers in Canadian federalism would be able to 'meet global economic challenges'. The contributors, both academics and practitioners, in the main gave a positive evaluation. Concerning the second charge, Bakvis and Chandler (1987a) point out that, contrary to what they see as Laski's rather premature prediction, federalism was alive and well, and this *regardless* of its concrete constitutional organization.[17]

In *both* cases, the federalist 'rebuttal', in its juxtaposition of unitary and federal political systems, appears to target only Laski's contentious and well-publicized generic statement that federalism was obsolete and hence its 'epoch over' (1939: 367). It does *not*, however, take seriously the insinuation of the epigraph, namely that there can be significant differences *among* federations, a more centralized form being better suited to confront 'giant capitalism'.

Purpose and Structure of the Study

Against the backdrop of the preceding discussion, it is my aim to examine the extent to which the institutional adjustment of federal countries to the process of economic globalization varies and to establish its cause. 'Institutional adjustment' is operationalized as the role of component governments in the negotiation as well as the domestic ratification and/or implementation of the international trade treaties on which economic regionalism is based. Preferential trade agreements themselves are conceptualized as the state response to economic globalization.

The federal states that will be compared are Germany and Canada, considered as occupying the centralized and decentralized poles, respectively, on a continuum of OECD federations.[18] *If* any difference among the formal and informal state responses to the conclusion of such treaties were to be observed, it certainly would have to be discerned among the two federal 'extremes'.[19] There are two possible scenarios as 'the state' tries to regain some measure of control over 'the market' via macro-regional integration schemes. First, if federalism is indeed an obstacle at large, then we should find that the same problems and delays exist in both Germany and Canada as they ratify and/or implement international trade treaties. Second, if instead the argument about the degree of centralization also holds for federations, then we should expect to see more difficulties and delays in Canada than in Germany.

The former finding would breathe new life into the sweeping 'obsolescence thesis' and would be less assuring for those stressing the general *economic* advantages of federalism over a unitary 'state' form (scenario 1). Alternatively, the latter outcome gives more credence to Laski's qualification contained in the epigraph and would seem to weaken the position that a high degree of decentralization manifest in a federal constitution does not significantly infringe on the 'flexibility' of the institutional adjustment to economic globalization (scenario 2).

The structure of the investigation is as follows. Chapter 2 begins with Cerny's discussion of globalization and its consequences for 'the state' (1995), and links it to the role of regional integration as an institutional state response to globalization (Coleman and Underhill, 1998; Mattli, 1999). Based on a review of the major tenets of Fiscal Federalism, it then develops three hypotheses about the conditions under which particular formerly national public sector functions are likely to be supranationalized. In Chapter 3, the analytical limitations of Fiscal Federalism are taken as a starting point to introduce the model of domestic institutional mediation between globalization and the policy outcome as developed by Garrett and Lange (1996). Within that model, I subsequently isolate the constitutional role of component governments as institutional veto players, which possibly are involved in both the negotiations of an international economic treaty, as well as its subsequent domestic ratification and implementation. Finally, I construct the analytical framework for the empirical investigation by integrating the theoretical insights of the two chapters.

On this basis, Chapter 4 investigates the role played by the German Länder in the country's ratification of the Single European Act (SEA) in 1986 and the Treaty on European Union (TEU), the so-called Maastricht Treaty, in 1992. Chapter 5 first contrasts it with the influence of the Canadian provinces on the implementation procedures for the bilateral free trade agreement with the United States (CUSFTA) in 1988. In a second step, the chapter explores their part in the North American Free Trade Agreement (NAFTA) and its side agreements on labor (NAALC) and the environment (NAAEC). Chapter 6 briefly compares the subnational influence, or absence thereof, on the German/European and Canadian positions during the Uruguay Round of the GATT as a 'control case', since both countries ultimately signed the *same* trade treaty. It concludes with a review of the study's findings and suggests directions for future research that seem to follow from the present investigation.

Notes

1 For an illustration of different views on globalization, compare Falk (1997), Fitzgerald (1997) and Julius (1997). Helleiner (1997), in contrast, regards most current studies as too narrow. He recommends utilizing the analytical tools of the economic historian Fernand Braudel for the study of globalization, which would require a simultaneous analysis of different spatial dimensions, time frames and social perspectives.

2 A more systematic study of the phenomenon could organize, in a 'hierarchical' fashion, its economic, political, social and cultural aspects – and then explore the interaction between them according to different levels of analysis (Hülsemeyer, 2003).

3 The application of the terminology is not uniform in the literature. Keohane and Milner (1996) employ 'internationalization' in the manner in which others, for instance, Bernstein and Cashore (2000), use 'globalization'. Throughout this study, I will apply these terms interchangeably; both are understood merely in the economic sense.

4 'Economies of scale' mean that for different quantitative output levels of a 'product' (here the particular functions of the nation-state in the economy) the average costs of production will increase or decrease (so-called quantity dependency of costs).

5 However, this causality may not be entirely clear-cut within the European context. EC/EU integration since the single market program in 1986 to a certain degree is also a reflection of *already* increased intra-regional economic transactions, rather than of globalization *as such* (see Chapter 4).

6 As a corollary, if regional integration schemes are indeed a common reaction of states to globalization, what explains the marked variation in the degree of institutionalization, that is, the movement of PSFs upward, between, for instance, the EU and the NAFTA?

7 A quotation from the second of his ten hypotheses shall illustrate the point: 'Developments in economic sectors characterized predominantly by the production, exchange, or use of public goods and specific assets will be increasingly shaped and determined by the particular scale of those goods and assets, whether transnational, national, local, or somewhere in between'. The three corollaries immediately following the hypothesis aim to clarify the argument by distinguishing between public goods that require production processes 'at a global or international-regional scale'; those for which the scale of the goods structure 'remains broadly congruent with the territorial parameters of the national economy'; and those public goods that 'are relatively isolated from transnational market linkages' (1995: 622–3). Yet, *which* public goods fall under the respective corollaries is based more on anecdotal examples (environmental protection, public housing, subsistence farming) rather than a precise and systematic categorization.

8 While it is of course not welfare-optimal to shift *all* PSFs upward, this study will focus exclusively on their potential supranationalization for three reasons. First, economic regionalism is the empirically most significant 'state' response to the process of economic globalization. Second, the devolution of formerly national PSFs does not present a 'problem' insofar as a subnational level of government is unlikely to reject an increase in competencies – provided the necessary financial resources are forthcoming. Third, the privatization of PSFs is extremely rare empirically.

9 For instance, in 2000 intra-regional merchandise trade in Western Europe accounted for 67.8 per cent of the region's total merchandise exports; for North America, the equivalent figure is 39.8 per cent (WTO, 2001: 40).

10 This coincides with the realm of the *positive* Fiscal Federalism, namely to explore whether a governmental decision was indeed motivated by economic considerations (Wildasin, 1997).

11 Depending on the economic model being adopted, the groups primarily affected by internationalization thus defined are aligned either on the basis of factors of production (Stolper-Samuelson theorem) or along sectoral lines (Ricardo-Viner approach).

12 But note that the converse is not true. Not every bicameral system is necessarily federal. If unitary states are based on two chambers, then the regional chamber has exactly the same constituency, i.e. it is voted for nationally like the first chamber (parliament). For this reason, the Netherlands moved from a bicameral to a unicameral system, while in Italy the Senate still exists although it mirrors parliament even in party-political composition. Only federations can exhibit 'true' bicameralism – and therefore have institutional VPs – since the two houses are based on *differently* sized constituencies.

13 Tsebelis (1995) actually asserts that the number of institutional VPs is to be based exclusively on the constitutionally prescribed role of the second or upper chamber in the policy-making process.

14 Belgium did not become a federation until 1992–93, largely to accommodate differences between its Dutch speaking (Flames) and French speaking (Wallones) groups. Spain has 17 autonomous regions, but none the less remains a unitary state with 52 provinces. Austria, beside Germany the only traditional federation, did not accede to the EU until 1995.

15 It is notable that hardly any scholars from the rather centralized federations of Germany

and Austria saw the need to advance (English) contributions 'in defence of federalism'. Their treatments are for the most part 'merely' analytical, rarely normative.

16 It should be obvious that 'flexibility' has a positive connotation for Boeckelman. This understanding, however, is not shared unanimously in the literature; instead, one could conceive of 'stability', seen as the prevention of frequent and erratic change, as more important. Yet, this study is concerned with formal institutional adjustment, which is neither frequent nor erratic; in this sense, the negative implication of the term for some does not seem to hold here.

17 In more general terms, Saunders (1995: 61) points to the 'wide and widening variety of federal structures in systems around the world'.

18 According to the 2001 WTO international trade statistics (displaying 2000 figures), the two countries are economically globalized and regionalized to the following extent. *Germany* had with US$1873 billion clearly the highest GDP within Western Europe (US$8448 billion); the second placed UK exhibits a GDP of US$1415 (WTO, 2001: 63). Germany is also the leading merchandise trader in Western Europe, with exports accounting for 22.6 per cent (second-placed France: 12.2 per cent) and imports measuring 19.6 per cent (second-placed UK: 13.1 per cent) (WTO, 2001: 64). Intra-EU merchandise trade exhibits 61.8 per cent for exports and 59.1 per cent for imports (WTO, 2001: 65). *Canada* had a GDP of US$689 billion in 2000, compared to US$9896 for the United States (WTO, 2001: 47). Its merchandise trade displayed 87.3 per cent of its exports and 64.4 per cent of its imports with the USA (WTO, 2001: 48). Conversely, Canada was the United States' single largest trading *economy*, absorbing 22.9 per cent of its merchandise exports accounting for 19.0 per cent of its imports. As such, Canada is leading the European Union (21.1 per cent and 18.1 per cent) by a narrow margin (WTO, 2001: 49).

19 The argument coincides with the one made in a comparison of seven federal countries and the EU, in which Germany's adjustment to global and regional integration is dubbed as 'centralizing', whereas Canada falls under the category 'decentralizing' (see Lazar *et al.*, 2003).

Chapter 2

Globalization and the Adjustment of the Public Sector

Although studies on the process of globalization abound, Cerny (1995) has provided one of the few, if not the only, analysis to date that generates hypotheses on the implications of economic globalization for the future of the nation-state's role in the economy. He principally asserts that globalization forces state governments to continually adjust their political institutions to this process. In his terminology, the optimal 'political economies of scale' are changing, leading to a shift from the welfare state to the 'competition state'. This might happen at different speeds in various countries but he sees this development as principally inevitable, contending that the power of international business compels national governments into deregulation.

Two kinds of challenges may be brought forward against Cerny's treatment. First, it is contested in the literature that the end of the welfare state is indeed inevitable under conditions of economic globalization in principle, and with a view to the European context in particular (Pierson, 1996b; Feigenbaum *et al.*, 1998; Garrett, 1998). These explorations focus on the policy *outcome*, that is, on whether or not national governments actually do what Cerny claims they ought to. The route pursued in this study is slightly different. The *logic* of the shift to the competition state implicitly depends upon the interest of multinational corporations and international finance in the deregulation of the national welfare state. While the existence of such pressure is merely *assumed* rather than verified by Cerny, several studies indicate that business actors are simultaneously instrumental in bringing about reregulatory measures of various kinds at the supranational level (Cowles, 1995; Mayer, 1998; Mattli, 1999; Bornschier, 2000).

The second criticism concerns Cerny's hypotheses about the fate of various groups of public goods (regulatory, distributive and redistributive) after the demise of the welfare state. These propositions are formulated in a rather vague manner, rendering them virtually untestable in their present form. Yet, the analytical precision of Cerny's hypotheses can be extended by employing the economic subdiscipline of Fiscal Federalism, which is concerned with a welfare optimal assignment of public sector functions (stabilization, distribution, allocation) among different levels of government. It distinguishes between public goods with and without so-called purchased inputs (taxes and user fees). Among the latter, the theory also differentiates between impure and pure public goods (those for which costs and benefits can technologically be confined to a specific geographic area and those for which this is not possible). Since this public goods typology is more refined than Cerny's tripartite classification, it allows for the formulation of more concrete hypotheses.

The first section of the chapter delineates the process of globalization and its consequences for political authority, namely the national welfare state, as conceptualized by Cerny. The establishment of macro-regional integration schemes as a response to the alleged deregulation at the national level, as well as the role of the business community in bringing them about, is the topic of the second section. Since in this context the question of the exact conditions that facilitate the supranationalization of particular public sector functions arises, the third section outlines the principal argumentation of Fiscal Federalism; I generate three hypotheses from it with regard to the centralization of public sector functions under conditions of a globalized economy.

Changing Political Economies of Scale and the Competition State

Globalization: Operationalizing an Elusive Concept

Cerny defines globalization as a set of economic and political structures, which derive from the increasing structural differentiation of the goods and assets that form the basis of the international political economy (1995: 596).[1] More concretely, he is interested in the manner in which the changing character of both public and private goods as well as of specific and non-specific assets influences collective action at the intersection between political-institutional and market structures (1995: 597–8).

Following Olson (1965), public goods are characterized by their indivisibility and the subsequent problem of free riding, meaning that individuals have an incentive to benefit from a public good without contributing to the costs of its provision. Hence, the market would not produce public goods in efficient outcomes. Instead, the hierarchical nature of political authorities is required in order to recoup these costs through the imposition of taxes and user fees. In contrast, private goods allow the purchaser to exclude others from the good's use, hence to prevent free riding. Therefore, private goods can be provided in efficient outcomes by the market, since sellers are able to acquire their costs from *all* buyers of the good or service.[2]

'Political economies of scale' is the term Cerny uses to describe the political-institutional structures that are more or less efficient in carrying out the functions of political authority in the market, namely 'stabilizing, regulating, controlling, or facilitating particular economic activities' (1995: 599). Depending on the state function in the economy under consideration, and also depending on the level of technological development and market demand at a given point in time, these political economies of scale vary. He contends that:

> [o]ptimal political economies of scale therefore continually shift, adjusting to technological, sociological, and political change. Indeed, they have been shifting dramatically in the late twentieth century, both upward to the transnational and global levels and downward to the local level. In this more fluid environment, actors' choices have significant consequences for the changing structure of the state and, indeed, for the wider evolution of politics and society (1995: 599).[3]

In terms of categorizing the economic functions of the state, Cerny (1995: 608–9) follows Theodor Lowi's (1964) classical portrayal of three kinds of public policy. *Regulatory* public goods, which encompass the framework in which economic activity takes place, include, for example, a stable currency and property rights, as well as common weights and measures. *Productive/distributive* public goods refer to the direct activities of the respective state in the economy. Their 'productive' variant comprises especially the provision of infrastructure, both in a technical (like roads and railroads) and a non-technical (for instance, public education) sense, while characteristic of the 'distributive' element is full or partial ownership of certain industries.[4] Finally, *redistributive* public goods contain the means commonly associated with the welfare state, that is, health care services, employment policies, financial assistance for low-income families, and so on. Redistribution is a method of de-commodification; political authorities try to achieve an allocation of income that broadly reflects the social values of a given society, which would not be forthcoming by the pure workings of the market economy.[5]

The essential feature of the 'second industrial revolution', Cerny asserts, is that it brought about a convergence of economic-organizational and political-institutional structures in the modern nation-state. In this sense, 'public goods' in general, and redistribution in particular, are very much a national-level phenomenon. However, the process of globalization is now disintegrating the existing national political structures from the economic-organizational optima. The so-called third industrial revolution, marked by the widely known technological advances in transportation and communications, supposedly has changed the power balance between politics and economics in favor of the latter in several interrelated ways. First, it enhanced the number of tradable goods and services, most notably, but by no means exclusively, in the financial sector (Frieden and Rogowski, 1996). Second, this increase strengthened the leverage of multinational corporations as the primary owners of mobile factors of production (capital, technical know-how) *vis-à-vis* territorial actors, the possessors of largely immobile factors of production (land, labor).[6] Third and subsequently, the economies of scale for businesses magnified, while the principal organization of political authority in the form of the nation-state has for the most part remained unaltered.

The Advent of the Competition State

As a result of this increasing gap between global market structures and national political institutions, Cerny argues that the state is no longer in the position to provide the three categories of public goods outlined above in the way it used to, following the second industrial revolution. Because of the increased leverage of MNCs, regulatory public goods have largely given way to competitive deregulation between nation-states in order to attract foreign direct investment (FDI) and production sites. This, however, has wider ramifications beyond the aspect of deregulation, as the – previously national – regulatory framework *itself* has the function of a public good. As regards the pressure on productive/distributive public goods, governments now focus on enhancing the economic attractiveness of their collectivities by investing in technical infrastructure and post-secondary education.[7] Moreover, states with traditions of full or partial public ownership of certain industries and service sectors like France and Germany are abandoning their shares in favor of the 'marketization' of these sectors, benefiting from the short-term easing of their fiscal crises that comes with it. Politicians increasingly see their role as active promoters of their respective constituencies *vis-à-vis* business interests, as numerous foreign 'trade missions' on all levels of government amply illustrate. Finally, in order to do so and to entice FDI and MNCs, Cerny asserts that the extent to which redistributive public goods can still be provided is being severely undermined, since they are often perceived as being responsible, through increasing labor costs, for reducing the incentives for productive investment.

Thus, in all aspects of government involvement in the economy, the process of globalization leads to divergence between the nation-state as the primary level of political authority and the increasing size of the market that is supposed to be influenced through different kinds of public goods. The result of these developments in general, and the abolition of redistributive public goods in particular, is a shift away from the national welfare state, whose essence is what Ruggie (cf. 1998: ch. 2) has termed 'embedded liberalism', that is, the combination of domestic regulation and international free trade. The increased domestic costs of maintaining redistributive public goods have led to the fiscal crisis of the national welfare state, exacerbated by the structural consequences of deregulation.

Together, these forces limit the capacity to insulate national economies, leading to the emergence of the 'competition state'.[8] Its two main features are: first, the reduction of government spending, not only for budgetary reasons, but in order to avoid the crowding out of private investment through public borrowing; and second, the deregulation of economic activities (see Figure 2.1).

Cerny sees the advent of the competition state as resulting from the policy changes that the process of globalization forces onto the political agenda. First, a shift takes place from macroeconomic to microeconomic interventionism, especially toward deregulation and industrial policy. Second, politicians pursue the 'competitive' advantage of their constituencies rather than a 'comparative' one; in other words, the concept of strategic industries and so-called national champions is given up. Third, the de-commodification

Figure 2.1 Argumentation of Cerny (1995)

of economic activities in order to achieve a more equitable distribution of income gives way to the active promotion of profitability in both public and private industries. Fourth, the sole imperative of monetary policy is inflation control, given the importance of monetary stability for both foreign investors and the locational choices of MNCs (Cerny, 1997: 258–63).

Hence, a paradox accompanying the process of globalization, according to Cerny, is that one would expect it to lead to a global economy *and* polity, that is, a new convergence of market-economy and political authority (1995: 618–21). Instead, globalization is also creating fragmentation, with *some* states, based on their economic capabilities, being better able and more willing to maintain elements of the welfare state than are others. Cerny conceptualizes three possible versions of the competition state. The original model, exemplified in the traditions of France, Japan and the south-east Asian newly industrialized countries, is based on strong state technocratic leadership and employs considerable intervention in market outcomes. On the opposite end of the spectrum, the orthodox model of the competition state is characterized by free-market economic liberalism of the Anglo-American variety. With its focus on deregulation, its ideology figured most prominently during the Thatcher and Reagan years of the 1980s. Finally, the continental European (and Scandinavian) neo-corporatist version of the competition state falls in between the Japanese and the Anglo-American models. The tripartite coordination of economic policies between government, business organizations and unions is crucial for its operation; neo-corporatist arrangements are more concerned with redistributive welfare provisions than is the case for the Anglo-American variant (Cerny, 1997: 263–8).[9]

Cerny holds that the interaction of these three models generates new political pressures for convergence around any one of them but considers the Anglo-American neoliberal model the prime candidate, since the competition state is mostly engaged in 'competitive de-regulation and creeping liberalization' (1997: 273–4). Although deregulation usually involves some form of reregulation, transnational settings for this purpose take time to be built. The function of the EU as such a framework, Cerny argues, is a point of ideological contention between the advocates of deregulation and reregulation (1991: 194). Here the interconnection between the emergence of the competition state and macro-regional integration schemes as political-institutional consequences of economic globalization becomes evident.

After the Demise of the Welfare State: Where to?

Cerny's argumentation has two cornerstones. First, he sees the shift from the welfare state to the 'competition state' as *inevitable*; this development follows logically for him from changing optimal 'political economies of scale' associated with the process of economic globalization. This assertion rests on the premise that governments have no choice but to institute deregulatory changes because of the pressure exerted through the increased power of MNCs and international investors. Whether these economic players indeed have an interest in the type of adaptation proposed by Cerny is *assumed* rather than empirically evidenced. Instead, as will be elaborated upon in the next section, reaping the benefits of a more open and deregulated economy depends on similar conditions among the main trading partners and free access to those markets. Since different national regulations often take the form of non-tariff barriers, business interests may not merely lie in dismantling aspects of the national welfare state but simultaneously in the conclusion of international treaties that try to secure this access and provide common regulations (Mattli, 1999).[10]

Second, if national deregulation is indeed on the rise, what happens to those public goods that will then no longer be provided by the welfare state? Since the concept of *changing* 'political economies of scale' analytically includes the *reassignment* of public sector functions to new, now 'optimal', levels of government, Cerny generates ten hypotheses with various corollaries regarding the various governmental levels likely to provide different kinds of public goods in the future (1995: 621–5). However, these hypotheses are formulated in such an ambiguous manner that they are not testable. An excerpt from the second of his ten hypotheses shall illustrate the point:

> Developments in economic sectors characterized predominantly by the production, exchange, or use of public goods and specific assets will be increasingly shaped and determined by the particular scale of those goods and assets, whether transnational, national, local, or somewhere in between.

The three corollaries immediately following the hypothesis aim to clarify the argument by distinguishing between public goods that require production processes 'at a global or international-regional scale'; those for which the scale of the goods structure 'remains broadly congruent with the territorial parameters of the national economy'; and those public goods that 'are relatively isolated from transnational market linkages' (1995: 622–3). Yet, *which* public goods fall under the respective corollaries is based more on anecdotal examples (environmental protection, public housing, subsistence farming) rather than a precise and systematic categorization.[11] In addition, Cerny's thesis of *changing* optimal political economies of scale logically requires that an assignment of public sector functions can be determined in the first place, that is, *before* the impact of globalization occurs. I submit in the third section of this chapter that the economic subdiscipline of Fiscal Federalism provides the analytical means to do so, as well as to extrapolate its logic and formulate testable hypotheses for conditions of economic globalization that also include redistributive policies.

Generalizing about Regional Integration

As the phenomenon of economically motivated macro-regional integration has taken root since the 1980s within and beyond industrialized countries, Mattli (1999) conducted one of the first systematic *comparative* explorations to establish commonalities among them.

Mattli's Argumentation: Two Puzzles

The purpose of Mattli's work is to explain the variation among regional integration schemes, understood as voluntary agreements between states 'to the extent that authority over key areas of national policy is shifted toward the supranational level' (1999: 1). He asserts that a general logic of macro-regional integration exists, hence, that the proliferation of integration schemes can be organized in an orderly fashion. Two puzzles arise in this context, which Mattli sets out to analyze in his study. First, what accounts for the ultimate success or failure of different macro-regional integration projects? He operationalizes 'success' as the degree to which treaty provisions are actually implemented into rules and regulations, since it is at this stage where several integration schemes have failed. Second, and closely related, if a macro-region is successful, under which conditions do 'outsiders' that encounter negative economic effects either join (that is, become belated 'insiders') or attempt to form a counter-union?[12]

Mattli proposes that certain demand and supply conditions must be fulfilled in order for a regional integration scheme to have a high likelihood of being successfully implemented. In terms of the demand side, he extrapolates from the contributions of property rights theory, economic history, and new institutional economics for the process of macro-regional integration. A combination of these three approaches suggests that 'as new technologies increase the scope of markets beyond the boundaries of a single state, actors who stand to gain from wider markets will seek to change an existing structure in order to realize these gains to the fullest extent' (1999: 46). Consequently, regional institution building can be understood as an attempt to internalize within a group of countries the externalities accruing from cross-border economic exchange.[13]

The potential economic costs of relying on foreign markets range from differing rates of inflation and currency devaluation to non-tariff barriers like distinct technical standards.[14] This has two implications: first, it raises the rationale for a macro-regional governance structure, that is, a framework that actually captures the geographically extended market it is supposed to manage. Second, the pressure for the supranationalization of rules and regulations governing economic exchange will come from the *market actors* that stand to benefit from the reduced risks associated with it.[15] They have played a crucial role in actively promoting the establishment of supranational regulations, aimed at replacing those at the national level, in both Europe and North America.

Beneficiaries of Macro-regional Integration: The Role of Business

In the EU, business interests have been organized since the early 1980s through the European Roundtable of Industrialists (ERT), which encompassed the CEOs of some of Europe's largest companies, including, among others, Siemens, Olivetti, GEC, Daimler Benz, Fiat and Bosch (Mattli, 1999: 77). Formed under the joint leadership of Volvo's then CEO Pehr Gyllenhammar and Philip's Wisse Dekker, its purpose was to press for an EU-wide standardization of rules and regulations governing market exchange, hence setting the agenda for a relaunch of EU integration.[16] This initiative was taken against the backdrop of 'Eurosclerosis', as the stalemate in EU economic integration during the 1970s and early 1980s was termed.[17] It was particularly harmful because mutual economic interdependence among the then twelve member states, which at the time already constituted the world's largest market with 340 million consumers, had grown dramatically. The ERT identified six areas (internal market, infrastructure, technology, jobs, environment and finance) for which it considered a common regulatory framework as crucial for reducing obstacles to growth within the EU; the establishment of a Community industrial policy was also seen as necessary (Cowles, 1995: 505–9).

The European Commission closely consulted with the Roundtable, drawing on its proposals in developing the so-called 1985 White Paper, calling for the creation of a single market (Cowles, 1995: 15). In the context of an Intergovernmental Conference establishing the details, this led, accompanied by much publicized threats of ERT members to relocate their companies outside the EU if the single market program were not adopted, to the signing of the SEA by the European Council in February 1986.[18]

In North America, a bilateral free trade agreement between the USA and Canada (CUSFTA) had been in place since 1989. Given that about 70 per cent of Mexico's (and Canada's) exports went to the United States, incoming Mexican President Salinas, was determined to end the country's traditional policy of import substitution by instituting wide-ranging domestic economic reforms, and proposed to negotiate a free trade agreement with the United States in June 1990.[19] US companies were attracted by the prospect of freer access to Mexico's 90 million consumers and a liberalization of the country's investment rules to take further advantage of its low labor costs in their competition with European and Japanese rivals (Shoch, 2000: 122). As a consequence, 'almost all major umbrella organizations representing big business' [as well as] 'small and medium-sized businesses ... vigorously supported' concluding the agreement (Mattli, 1999: 180). The Canadian government was initially not interested at all in taking part, since it already had secured the CUSFTA in 1989. However, it joined the talks, bowing to domestic business pressure (Mayer, 1998: 48).[20]

Concluding Regional Integration Schemes: Governments as Suppliers

Mattli stresses that the demand by business alone is not sufficient for the successful completion of such a scheme; instead, three supply conditions also have to be met. First, political leaders in the countries involved must have the *willingness* to surrender part of their national powers to a supranational governance structure. Politicians are conceptualized as preferring national autonomy and the will to stay in power, with the latter aspect being seen as a function of their ability to manage the domestic economy. Hence, Mattli asserts that they face a potential trade off between these two goals if a prolonged recession is threatening their reelection chances. Only then are they likely to consider giving up competencies to the supranational level in order to enhance national economic performance and thereby attempt to stay in office.

Second, even if politicians are willing to shift formerly domestic regulatory powers to the macro-regional level, they may not have the *ability* to do so because of two collective action problems. These are the so-called Prisoners' Dilemma, the standard case of externalities, and, even more significant for macro-regional integration, coordination games. The conceptual problem of the Prisoners' Dilemma is the difference between individual and collective rationality. Although two or more states would jointly benefit from the establishment of common rules and regulations, each of them has an incentive to defect, assuming that the other partners comply. Since the problem of achieving the collectively favorable outcome is largely one of communication, that is, information about the others' willingness to obey, this difficulty can be overcome through so-called commitment institutions that oversee and enforce rule adherence. This is the second, albeit *weak*, supply condition; it facilitates compliance but cooperation might occur even without such institutions, as evidenced by the absence of equivalents to the European Commission and the European Court of Justice in other successful macro-regions.

Third, and important for macro-regional integration, is the *strong* supply condition, which is a consequence of so-called coordination games. In contrast to the Prisoners' Dilemma, the question here is not *how* a collectively favorable outcome can be achieved but *which* of different possible alternatives will be attained. Since the latter vary in the relative distribution of the benefits among participants, states have opposing preferences about these results. On this basis, Mattli holds, successful regional integration projects require the presence of a benevolent hegemon for two reasons. First, it serves as the focus for the standardization of rules and regulations, as the aggregate regional costs of converging around the regional leader are lower than adopting the standards of any economically less significant member state. Second, given that *any* of the various possible cooperative outcomes raise distributional issues, the economic hegemon can ease them by virtue of its financial capabilities, serving as the regional 'paymaster'.

The above demand and supply conditions, although developed to resolve the first puzzle, i.e. the variation of successful and failed regional integration projects, also have a bearing on the second puzzle. If 'outsiders' face negative externalities from an existing macro-region, among them the relative loss of market access and investment diversion, they can either attempt to join the union causing the negative externalities or, in case the application for membership is rejected, form a counter-union. Mattli calls these options the first and second integrative responses, respectively.

Existing PTAs will only admit new members if these are either likely to make a net positive contribution to the union's budget or if their continued exclusion were costlier for the region than acceptance, for instance, because of the threat of economically motivated migration into the union. If an applicant does not meet either of these criteria, a counter-union might be formed. In this case, the same demand and supply conditions apply in order for it to be as successful as for the original union.[21]

Mattli tests his framework by examining several integration projects in the nineteenth and twentieth centuries. He considers both European integration since the signing of the Single European Act and the NAFTA as the most recent successful macro-regions.[22] Yet, this finding raises an additional analytical question.

Institutional Disparity: The Third Puzzle

While Mattli convincingly makes the case for the demand and supply conditions that distinguish successful and failed PTAs, categorizing the EC/EU and the NAFTA in the same way clouds their substantial difference in the governance structures established to integrate the respective regional markets. Put differently, considerable institutional variation exists *among* successful integration schemes.

First, in terms of the *demand* side for regional integration, international business actors pursued different strategies in the EU and NAFTA. The former wanted to see a macro-regional regulatory framework established that in large measure would mimic the continental European national welfare states. In contrast, their North American counterparts, although heavily divided into sectoral lobby groups and pressuring for transition periods between five and fifteen years, in principle preferred regulations that resemble Cerny's concept of the deregulatory competition state. Second, Mattli accounts only for those market actors that are in favor of supranational rules and regulations, as they stand to benefit from increased economies of scale and reduced transaction costs. He excludes the forces, which presumably have a vested interest in resisting the transfer of domestic regulatory powers to the macro-regional level, for they ultimately failed in their endeavor. Politicians, facing prolonged domestic recession and thereby the threat of electoral defeat, disregard their concerns and give up domestic autonomy to survive politically (Mattli, 1999: 51). Reducing the actors on the demand side to business, however, leaves two aspects of variation unexamined. To begin, it remains unaccounted for whether opposition to the proposed integration scheme existed at all, that is, whether there was substantial resistance to the scheme. Furthermore, *if* this were indeed the case, opposition need not be limited to blocking the treaty altogether. Instead, the supposed adversaries may in part attempt to *influence* the outcome in their favor through modifying or 'softening' the treaty provisions preferred by the business actors.

Third, concerning what Mattli terms the *supply* side, he holds that politicians not only have to demonstrate their willingness to conclude a regional integration scheme. They are most likely to face difficulties in their *ability* to do so, attributed primarily to coordination problems *among* member states in agreeing on the precise rules and regulations of the project. What this treatment overlooks is that the potential of governments to supranationalize public sector functions and to implement such commitments domestically can vary considerably among member states with different constitutional environments; this logically would apply *prior* to coordination games at the macro-regional level.

While the analytical concern posed by these three aspects will be addressed in Chapter 3, they all beg the question as to the conditions under which the provision of what public goods is likely to be transferred upward from the realm of the national welfare state to a macro-regional level. This would thereby increase the precision of Cerny's hypotheses. Examining the assignment of public sector functions among different levels of government is the prerogative of the economic subdiscipline of Fiscal Federalism. It is, therefore, this theoretical approach that we now turn to.

Toward a Theory of Regulatory Change: Fiscal Federalism as a Building Block[23]

An Economic Approach to Federalism

The research interest of the economic subdiscipline of Fiscal Federalism is the particular allocation of public sector functions among different levels of government which secures the achievement of the economic welfare optimum, defined as the *simultaneous* fulfillment of an efficient allocation of resources *and* an equitable distribution of income.[24] Attaining the welfare optimum makes some form of government involvement imperative, since without it the market economy would suffer from three deficiencies.

First, fiscal and monetary policies are necessary to combine high output and employment with stability. Second, in the absence of a public sector, misallocations, externalities and market imperfections occur, which *prevent* an efficient allocation of resources and necessitate the production and provision of public goods. Third, even assuming an efficient allocation of resources, this does not guarantee an equitable, that is, socially desirable, distribution of income; in fact, it would be mere coincidence. Thus, the public sector has to resolve the problems of stabilization, distribution and allocation (Oates, 1991: 49). The distinction between these three public sector functions serves only an analytical purpose; in reality, they are highly interrelated (Oates, 1972: xv).

Fiscal Federalism has a *normative* component, as it employs an economic rationale to examine how governments *should* behave in order to accomplish the economic welfare optimum.[25] This can be seen as principally realistic, as all governments will, in order to stay in power, strive to achieve *some* form of allocative efficiency and determine the distribution of income. The distinction between governments in different societies/ideologies is one of degree, not of kind.[26] The relative importance of efficiency and distribution, although the former is to some extent a prerequisite for the latter, depends on the values of a given society (see Figure 2.2).[27]

Figure 2.2 Argumentation of (Normative) Fiscal Federalism

G = (economic) globilization
COPES = changing optimal political economies of scale
RPSF = reassignment of public sector functions

The economic meaning of federalism is different from the political application of the term. For fiscal federalists, it is not relevant whether the decision making at a particular governmental level is based on delegated or constitutionally guaranteed authority. Instead, for economists what matters is the extent to which the allocation decisions *themselves* reflect the preferences of citizens within a given jurisdiction.[28] Hence, in economic terms all systems are federal; the distinction between them is one of degree, not of kind. Therefore, the discipline begins by analytically distinguishing between the poles of complete centralization and decentralization, yet assuming in both cases a single currency and the absence of constraints on the free movement of goods and services. The sole variance between the two forms then is the *extent* of centralization of the public sector.

The Assignment of Public Sector Functions among Levels of Government

The economic rationale for centralization The *stabilization* function of the public sector consists of two components: monetary and fiscal policy. Fiscal federalism proposes that the responsibility for the exercise of both forms of macroeconomic policy must rest with the central government. Regarding *monetary policy*, if each level of government were to create and destroy money, there would exist a powerful incentive for decentralized governments to finance their purchases of goods and services with newly created money rather than burdening their constituencies with taxation. In terms of *fiscal policy*, which encompasses revenue as well as expenditure programs, decentralized governments face serious constraints on the employment of counter-cyclical measures because of the high mobility of capital as well as the 'openness' of local economies. They export and import relatively large shares of the goods they produce and consume, meaning that any additional spending by a particular decentralized jurisdiction which can hardly be restrained within its borders and will, therefore, mostly benefit 'foreigners'.

The optimal resolution of the second public sector task, the *distribution* problem, which denotes the socially desired redistribution of income among individuals and collectivities, depends largely upon constraints on the mobility of residents. The fewer impediments that exist, the more likely that any determined income redistribution in one jurisdiction will lead to an outmigration of high-income earners and an influx of low-income earners; this resulting loss of the necessary financial basis will eventually render the original policy impossible. Hence, the income redistribution function is also to be centralized, since the geographically higher the level of government responsible, the lower is the mobility of residents, creating the type of externality that is the very source of under-provision of assistance to low-income households in a decentralized system.

Individual income redistribution is favorable over collective, that is, regional, allotment. The rationale behind this claim is that in every poor community there also live some wealthy persons, and vice versa. Thus, regional income redistribution through intergovernmental grants will always exhibit less optimal results compared to income redistribution on an individual basis. None the less, political constraints may render such grants the only feasible and effective redistributive policy; for achieving the welfare optimum, regional redistribution is better than no redistribution at all (Oates, 1972: 81).

While the decision on the proper governmental level is straightforward for the stabilization and distribution functions, the resolution of the *allocation* problem is more complex.[29] Here the responsibility of the public sector is twofold. First, government agencies exercise control over the economy through the use of *regulatory* measures that prescribe various forms of activity for individuals and firms in the private sector. Second, if levels of output are *not* forthcoming in efficient quantities through the operation of free markets, they directly produce and/or provide public goods.

In terms of regulatory measures, the imposition of environmental standards for pollutants is a typical case for intervention by central authorities, if localities are to take into account the effects of their polluting activities on those outside their borders. But even if pollution is rather geographically limited, national minimum standards avert destructive inter-regional competition. Analogous to the often cited phenomenon of tax competition between jurisdictions, state and local authorities may otherwise compete with one another through reducing environmental standards to lower the costs for prospective business enterprises (Oates, 1977: 59–61).

In contrast to regulatory measures, the production and/or provision of public goods and services requires so-called *purchased inputs*, meaning government revenues in the form of taxes and user fees. Two kinds of public goods with purchased inputs exist: *pure* and *impure* ones. In the case of the former, the benefits of their provision unavoidably extend to all communities; external security is one of the standard cases in this vein. For impure public goods, by contrast, it is *technically* possible to confine their benefits and costs to particular constituencies; classical examples include the police service, waste management and fire protection.[30]

It follows that Fiscal Federalism suggests a centralized provision of pure public goods, as decentralization would inevitably result in inefficient levels of output. For impure public goods, however, there is likely to be a solution in greater decentralization. This is so because the criterion of economic efficiency for the allocation function is defined as the mix of output that best reflects the preferences of the individuals who make up any given society.[31]

The economic rationale for decentralization The advantage of a decentralized solution for impure public goods over unitary provision is the potential for enhancing allocative efficiency through a closer reflection of different residential preferences. Tiebout (1956) has famously suggested that, assuming varied levels of public goods provision among different adjacent municipalities, residents may move between them, thereby 'voting with their feet' and over time creating localities with relatively homogeneous preference structures among the populace.[32] Yet, Fiscal Federalism points out that several trade-offs need to be taken into account.

In the *ideal case* – the analytical starting point of any economic model – the structure of governments allows for a *perfect correspondence*, that is, the jurisdiction which determines the level of provision for each public good includes precisely the set of individuals who consume the good. This would lead to a Pareto efficient level of output.[33] Fiscal Federalism releases the conceptual restrictions of the ideal model along three lines: the variability of group size; inter-jurisdictional externalities; and the costs of collective decision-making.

The first aspect addresses the possibility that the same impure public good, for instance crime protection, can technologically be consumed in varied jurisdictional sizes. On the one hand, depending on the technical character of the good itself, economies of scale may allow cheaper provision through joint consumption; in other words, the greater the number of consumers the better. On the other hand, if individuals have different preferences regarding the level of provision, joint consumption constitutes a welfare loss for either side, which tends to increase the larger the group.[34] The two factors that determine the optimal size of fiscal decentralization under these conditions are: (i) the actual degree of diversity of individual demands; and (ii) the extent to which consumers with similar tastes live in geographical groupings. In the aforementioned 'Tiebout world' the mere existence of varied preferences for public goods provision among individuals would not be sufficient. Only if these differences also translate into geographical concentration is a local provision of the impure public good economically advantageous.

Second, in terms of inter-jurisdictional externalities, it is desirable to internalize them, since otherwise an incentive exists for free riding. *Inter alia*, the inclusion of external effects in the calculation exhibits a tendency for larger rather than smaller community governments for the provision of impure public goods. Finally, the implication in the ideal model is that there should be a separate level of government corresponding to the optimal group size for *each* public good.[35] Even if this were politically feasible, there is an economic incentive *not* to do so because of the mostly fixed costs of public decision making. Thus, where optimal-sized jurisdictions are roughly the same, a single level of government is desirable (Oates, 1972: 46–9).

Releasing the analytical assumptions of the ideal model illustrates that in the absence of perfect correspondence, trade-offs exist between the gains from independent governmental levels and their increased decision-making costs. While the technical nature of impure public goods is a necessary condition for their decentralized provision in general, these trade-offs determine exactly *which level* of decentralization (municipal, metropolitan or Land/provincial) is welfare optimal.

The discussion demonstrates that for impure public goods also Fiscal Federalism can generate propositions about the welfare optimal level of government for their provision. Yet, as their complexity requires the determination of the trade-off for each of the goods separately, I exempt them from the ensuing discussion.

Hypothesizing the Institutional Adjustment to Globalization

The economic logic of Fiscal Federalism's normative propositions can be applied to the environment of a globalized economy. On the basis of the preceding argumentation, three hypotheses about the shift of centralized public sector functions can be formulated.

In terms of the *stabilization function*, Fiscal Federalism proposes the centralization of monetary and fiscal policy for two reasons. First, decentralized levels of government resemble highly open economies; since this means that they are also faced with a high degree of mobility of financial capital, monetary policy must be centralized. Second, as open economies exhibit strong mutual interdependence through the associated level of cross-border business activity, any attempt to pursue anticyclical policies would be rendered ineffective; this creates an incentive to centralize fiscal policy. The process of economic globalization allegedly enhances both factors beyond national frontiers.

Hypothesis 1: The more open national economies are, the more likely that monetary and fiscal policies will be shifted to a supranational level encompassing the nation-states for which these conditions apply.

Regarding the *distribution function*, Fiscal Federalism advocates a centralized provision because the mobility of residents tends to be greater the smaller the jurisdiction is. Income redistribution by one decentralized jurisdiction would probably lead to an outmigration of wealthy and an influx of low-income inhabitants, thereby defeating the initial purpose of the distributive policy. Supposedly, global market conditions have facilitated individual mobility beyond national borders.

Hypothesis 2: The higher individual mobility beyond national borders, the more likely that individual and/or regional income redistribution will be shifted to a supranational governmental level encompassing the nation-states for which this condition applies.

With respect to the *allocation function*, Fiscal Federalism distinguishes between public goods for which the provision can technically be limited to subsets of society and those for which this is not feasible. Impure public goods can include different levels of decentralized governments whereby the concrete choice depends on an assessment of the trade-offs involved. By contrast, pure public goods with purchased inputs and a number of regulatory public goods are to be provided centrally, for decentralized levels of government will fall short of providing a Pareto-efficient output. Presumably, global economic pressures have augmented the necessity for enhancing efficient resource allocation beyond national frontiers.

Hypothesis 3: The higher the pressures for efficient resource allocation, the more likely that the provision of the regulatory as well as pure public goods with purchased inputs will be shifted to a supranational level among the nation-states for which these conditions are valid.

The hypotheses suggest that the public sector is by no means static. Instead, its continuing evolution has led to two marked changes in the vertical structure of government. One is the establishment of metropolitan area governments in 'global cities' (Brenner, 1998); the other is the creation of PTAs with varying degrees of integration, most prominently the European

Union and the North American Free Trade Agreement. It is this latter concept of macro-regional integration that will be explored in detail in Chapters 4 and 5 of this study.

Qualifications

Although the preceding discussion suggests that Fiscal Federalism is a viable candidate to theorize about changing optimal political economies of scale, three clarifications are in order. First, the divergence between Cerny and Fiscal Federalism is an *analytical* one, not necessarily an empirical one. Cerny's depiction of the significance of the Anglo-American version of the competition state constitutes a *special case* within a fiscal federalist framework. It must be examined *empirically* whether the process of globalization is indeed leading to a convergence on the Anglo-American neoliberal or rather the European neo-corporatist model of the competition state. By contrast, the section on macro-regional integration implies that continued divergence between the two variants might be the most likely scenario.

Second, the economic meaning of federalism insinuates that Fiscal Federalism is not concerned with the mediating influence of domestic institutional settings. In this vein, the hypotheses draw a causal link from economic globalization *directly* to the conditions for the supranationalization of formerly domestic public sector functions. This, however, is not to say that constitutional provisions are irrelevant to the discipline. On the contrary, Fiscal Federalism appears to imply that the more decentralized a political system, the more difficult the political-institutional adaptation will be.

Third, Fiscal Federalism does not claim to reveal *ex post* the underlying interests of political actors; instead, it simply follows economic logic to its conclusion.[36] Thus, its prescriptions are normative; they outline how governments *should* (re)assign the responsibilities for various public sector functions, *if* they wish to achieve the Pareto optimum. While the latter is generally a realistic assumption for governments accountable to the electorate, whether or not they actually are *willing* to and/or *can* follow these prescriptions in the short to medium term is an empirical question.

The conceptual resolution of these three qualifications, as well as the earlier one about the different degrees of regional integration, will be combined into one analytical framework and developed in Chapter 3. In accordance with the two criticisms of Cerny's work advanced in this chapter, the ensuing discussion will be conducted with an eye to the supranationalization of public sector functions under conditions of economic globalization.

Notes

1 Though 'goods' and 'assets' are often used interchangeably, the former term mostly refers to commodities, while the latter tends to represent production facilities.

2 A similar rationale underlies the relation between specific and nonspecific assets (Cerny, 1995: 599–601). For reasons of simplification, I limit the analysis to public (and, hence indirectly, also private) goods. Lane (1995: 14–48) critically assesses the possibility of analytically separating private and public goods.

3 Note that in his view the necessity for change is not simply exogenously, that is, structurally, given. Cerny's emphasis on 'actors' choices' highlights the limitations that political decisions pose for future policy options. This so-called path dependency can also be seen as a means to address the potential circularity of an argumentation that mainly introduces globalization as a cause for institutional adjustment, yet has to present it as a consequence of deliberate political choice at the same time.

4 Recently, Cerny has suggested treating productive and distributive public goods as separate categories, arguing that while the former connotes the production, the latter refer to the delivery of the goods and services in question (1999: 196–7). This is similar to the distinction between the production and the provision of public goods, which under certain circumstances can be of significance in Fiscal Federalism (see n.35).

5 He sees the difference between productive/distributive public goods and redistributive ones precisely in the fact that the latter category is determined not by standards of economic efficiency but by normative considerations about fairness and justice (Cerny, 1999: 199). Yet, irrespective of the social values of a given society, income redistribution may in part simply be an economic necessity to achieve or maintain the fiscal federalist welfare optimum.

6 The term 'footloose capital' found its way also into the academic debate. Cerny argues that if MNCs, though operating internationally, remain embedded in national settings, this is only the case to the extent that certain forms of corporate organization still allow for competitive advantages in their respective sectors and markets (1996: 627). For an analysis of the existing differences between MNCs from the USA, Germany and Japan, and their continued respective national lock-ins, see Pauly and Reich (1997).

7 Scharpf (1994) postulates that the responsibility for these immobile factors of production may largely be devolved from national to subnational authorities, since an MNC's decision to establish a production site is made in favor of one subnational entity over another, rather than between nation-states. In contrast, Walz and Wellisch (1997) argue that decentralized levels of government are *only* able to provide immobile factors of production at optimal levels, *if* the agglomeration costs, that is, the costs for MNCs associated with the relocation of production sites, are negligible. Since this frequently is an unrealistic assumption, they maintain that in most cases in fact a centralized provision of the various public goods exhibits optimal levels of output.

8 Cerny also introduces the concept of the 'residual state', which he sees as the further consequence of the competition state, since the governmental functions carried out in the latter are de-commodified, hence they become 'residual' (1996: 632–7).

9 With his three forms of capitalism (US, European and Asian), Stubbs (1998) employs a conceptualization similar to Cerny. However, he asserts that the very distinctions between these three models will make it increasingly difficult to maintain a multilateral trade regime in the future. In other words, Stubbs does not foresee the eventual convergence around one form, but continued existence of all three. To what extent such a division between three types of capitalism actually clouds differences *within* the Anglo-American model (for instance, between Canada and the USA) is beyond the scope of this analysis.

10 In addition, the end of the welfare state has also been challenged from another angle. Feigenbaum *et al.*, in their examination of the political underpinnings of privatization, observe that 'jurisdictions facing similar environments have considerable leeway to shape their own specific responses' (1998: 26). The authors assert that the approaches put forth to explain the expansion of the welfare state also give leverage to investigate the tendency toward privatization. The three case studies explored by them (the United Kingdom, France and the USA) suggest counter-forces on both the international and the national level against the exogenous dismantling of the welfare state, among them nationalism. In

contrast, Pierson (1996a) questions whether theories of state growth can be utilized for an explanation of welfare state retrenchment. Comparing welfare retrenchment between the United Kingdom, the USA, Sweden and Germany, he posits that it is a common feature of all modern democracies that electoral considerations cause changes to welfare provisions to be only modest in character, since politicians strive for 'blame avoidance'. Clayton and Pontusson (1998) cast doubt on his findings for measurement reasons. They argue that Pierson did not account for changes in social welfare needs and the allocation of resources among individual programs. On this basis, they view Pierson's resilience thesis as less convincing. In sum, Feigenbaum *et al.* (1998) and Pierson (1996a) are more hesitant to announce the demise of the welfare state than Cerny is, although they acknowledge that 'privatization' or 'retrenchment' cannot be ruled out entirely. Yet, unlike Cerny, they do not propose what is likely to happen *once and if* welfare state functions are lost at the national level.

11 Note also that the hypotheses account for a potential reassignment only of *non*-welfare-related governmental functions. Cerny employs the meaning of changing political economies of scale solely to introduce the removal of (especially redistributive) national public goods, *without* allowing for their possible shift to a different (for example, supranational) governmental level.

12 Situating himself in the relevant literature, Mattli holds that most 'classical' theoretical approaches to regional integration in both political science (neofunctionalism, intergovernmentalism) and economics (customs union theory, optimal currency area theory) are insufficient to capture the *problématique* contained in the two puzzles. He views only Fiscal Federalism as being close to his own framework, as this economic subdiscipline goes beyond examining the levels of government best suited for different policies by providing 'more general reflections on the evolution of private markets and the creation of new institutions' (1999: 39). Although Mattli maintains that Fiscal Federalism presupposes a unified regional market, that is, it discounts the collective action problems involved in its establishment, he nonetheless agrees with its focus on economic factors for the creation of macro-regional institutions.

13 This emphasis on technological innovations as a crucial driving force in establishing new governance structures by enhancing the possibility for economic exchange to a larger geographical area corresponds to Spruyt's treatment of 'exogenous change' in bringing about the end of feudalism in Europe (1994).

14 Mattli also mentions political risks, such as the nationalization of foreign assets (1999: 47). In the context of the European and North American integration schemes, however, these aspects can be neglected.

15 This runs counter to standard economic theories that tend to take the political framework within which market actors find themselves as given, rather than to conceptualize these market actors as being actively engaged in driving political-institutional change.

16 Bornschier (2000: 29) emphasizes that, therefore, it was not European businesses as such but rather the 'transnational European business elite, with their considerable business stakes outside their headquarter countries', who were pushing for the single market project. In this context, note that Sweden, the home country of car manufacturer Volvo, was not even an EU member state at the time.

17 While 60 per cent of the countries' exports accounted for trade with each other (Keohane and Hoffmann, 1991), distinct national regulations, which the European Council (heads of state and government) was unable to overcome, prevented European companies from achieving enhanced economies of scale and reduced transaction costs. This, in turn, led to a considerable disadvantage *vis-à-vis* the mounting pressure from their US and Japanese competitors (Garrett, 1992).

18 The good relationship of ERT members with the French government, and especially with then President Mitterand, is considered crucial for having facilitated the abandonment of his initial 'socialism in one country' project in favor of a decidedly pro-EC regulatory stance. This policy shift paved the way for the successful conclusion of the SEA

negotiations, as the agreement now closely resembled the preferences of France and Germany (Garrett, 1992: 546–7).

19 He promoted the idea by emphasizing that 'Europe of 1992 will be the largest market of the world if we don't get an agreement' (quoted in Mayer, 1998: 45).

20 Because of the peculiar constitutional circumstances in the United States, Congress has to ratify international treaties concluded by the Administration. Therefore, an 'unprecedented marketing and lobbying campaign' by the business community, focusing on the economic competition emanating from deepened EU integration and Japan, was required to win Congressional approval in November 1993 (Mayer, 1998: 285).

21 Since the present study is concerned with the variation in governance structures among successful macro-regions, that is, among *insiders*, I will disregard Mattli's second puzzle in the remainder of the analysis.

22 Mattli considers the SEA a response to the competitive pressure of Japan and the United States, and the NAFTA a reply to fears of a 'fortress Europe', that is, an example of the second integrative response. Mayer (1998: 39) concurs with this assessment: 'Arguably we would not have a NAFTA (and before that a Canada-U.S. Free Trade Agreement [CUFTA]) had the Europeans not moved to create the European Union (EU)'.

23 Cerny has set down the development of a theory of regulatory change as his ultimate goal (1991: 174–6). Underhill (2000) asserts that IPE cannot meaningfully be studied without a theory of the state, the lack of which is a common feature of all theoretical approaches to date. In a different context, Strange (1996) suggested that her own 'anti textbook', as she labeled her seminal *States and Markets* (1994), should have emphasized 'political authorities' in the book's title rather than 'states' in order to stress that nation-states are not or are no longer the only relevant actors in IPE. Thus, a theory of regulatory change could fill the void identified by Underhill without taking the political institution of 'the state' as *a priori* given. For analytical purposes, however, it might prove useful to keep the two concepts separate. A theory of the state examines *which* functions 'the state' assumes over time, while a theory of regulatory change explores *where* these functions are located in different eras. Where the former goes beyond a narrow economic conception of public goods to include, for instance, identity and legitimacy, the latter moves beyond a narrow conception of 'the state' to encompass both different levels of government and non-governmental actors.

24 Note that the *purpose* of the Anglo-American version of the competition state is *not* the achievement of the economic welfare optimum, since with its emphasis on deregulation and liberalization it is concerned merely with efficient resource allocation but not with income distribution.

25 In addition to this assignment of *expenditure* functions, the vertical structure of *revenues* must be determined, which consists of two components: (i) tax-assignment, and (ii) intergovernmental grants. For an examination, see Oates (1972: chs 3 and 4). Cerny's depiction of public goods only covers the output, that is, the expenditure side, whereas the question of financing the production and provision of public goods is inevitably omitted.

26 In its *positive* variant, Fiscal Federalism empirically assesses to what extent its propositions hold in reality, that is, whether governmental actors actually *do* exhibit the policies fiscal federalist logic suggests they should. Put differently for the context of economic globalization, it explores the extent to which the political change we observe can be attributed to economic imperatives (Wildasin, 1997: 32).

27 Susan Strange (1994) has argued that the three major IPE ideologies differ in the *relative* importance that they attribute to the four basic values: wealth, security, equity and justice. As security considerations do not play a role in a fiscal federalist framework, societies can be seen as varying according to their focus on either wealth (efficient resource allocation) or equity (income redistribution).

28 In other words, it is less important *who* makes decisions. *If* the central government had perfect knowledge of sub-central preferences, all decisions could be centralized (Cremer *et al.*, 1997). In this hypothetical case, Fiscal Federalism would no longer have an object

of study, since its *problématique*, the optimal degree of decentralization, would be resolved. Yet, central governments are dependent on detecting individual preferences through elections; thus, the information will always be imperfect.

29 The meaning of 'public goods' in Fiscal Federalism differs from Cerny's usage of the term. The stabilization function is a regulatory public good for Cerny, whereas the distribution function equals his redistributive public goods, and the allocation function would most probably resemble his category of productive/distributive public goods. Put differently, Fiscal Federalism distinguishes between public *sector* and public *goods*. The former involves the three governmental functions of stabilization, distribution and allocation. The latter refers to the production and/or provision of governmental services under the allocation function only.

30 Ostrom and Ostrom (1977: 12) differentiate between the two independent attributes of 'exclusion' and 'jointness of use or consumption'. On the basis of this classification, they view both pure public goods and pure private goods as 'extreme case'. However, the authors include among the examples in their pure public goods category both national defense and fire protection. This differs from Fiscal Federalism's focus in that Ostrom and Ostrom are not concerned in their depiction with the variance in the *geographical extent* to which different public goods are in joint use and not exclusionary. Hence, for Fiscal Federalism national defense is a pure public good, while fire protection is an example of an impure public good.

31 This efficiency criterion does *not* apply to the stabilization problem, since monetary and fiscal policies are not matters of individual preferences. To the extent that the *level* of income distribution reflects the preferences within a given society, these values do not depend on a subset but on that society as a whole.

32 It is here where the origin of Fiscal Federalism in the US public finance context becomes obvious (Oates, 1977: 4). It should be noted that the subsequent public choice literature (cf. Mueller, 1979), which in part depicts itself as 'modern' political economy (Frey, 1978), is equally confined to the micro-regional realm of impure public goods with purchased inputs. Even more so, a 'Tiebout world' is only applicable on the local level, since moving costs (which increase with distance) as well as non-economic considerations for not 'voting with one's feet' (for instance, attachment to neighbors) are omitted.

33 Pareto efficiency means that the solution found is collectively optimal; it cannot be altered to enhance the benefits for one participating unit without making at least one other worse off at the same time.

34 As Ostrom *et al.* (1961) have illustrated, the technological character of some public goods may permit a solution of this trade-off problem by separating the production and provision of a public good. This allows for a combination of the gains from large-scale production and decentralized determination of the levels of consumption. Furthermore, Ostrom and Ostrom (1977) submit that the organization of collective 'consumption units', that is, the governmental providers of public goods, would enable these to contract out to competing public and private 'production units', thereby introducing an element of market efficiency into the public sector. The authors stress that the argument assumes the existence of either a voluntary agreement or mechanisms of conflict resolution between consumption and production units (1977: 19). However, given the potential for free riding mentioned earlier in this chapter, this *assumption* appears to be precisely the *problem* of collective action to be resolved.

35 One may view the development of single-function entities, the so-called special districts, in the United States as an attempt to create separate levels of government for the provision of different impure public goods with purchased inputs (Reischauer, 1977).

36 In this sense, like Cerny, it faces the same criticisms frequently leveled against functionalist argumentations. There are theoretically several institutional solutions possible that satisfy the criterion of Pareto efficiency. *Which* of these possibilities will be adopted is a matter of bargaining between the actors involved. Fiscal Federalism adds precision to the structural side of the argumentation and thereby facilitates more defined

hypotheses about the constraints within which actors can bargain in the era of economic globalization. Yet, as Dessler (1989) has pointed out, neither a theory focusing on the structure, nor one merely examining the bargaining processes among the actors involved can be fully explanatory.

Chapter 3

Tracing the Process of Institutional Mediation

The two main caveats of the fiscal federalist hypotheses identified in the previous chapter, namely that they are *normative* and draw a *direct* link from economic globalization to the 'optimal' government response (or reassignment of public sector functions), can only be addressed through tracing the adaptation process of domestic institutions. First, in this way it can be determined which domestic actors have the leverage to influence the government response to globalization pressures. Second, it allows the examination of whether the government change ultimately adopted was indeed motivated by economic considerations; this coincides with the purpose of *positive* fiscal federalism. Third, through tracing the process of institutional adjustment the domestic source(s) of cross-country variations and the extent to which public sector functions have been supranationalized can be explored.

Garrett and Lange (1996) have developed the only causal model to date on *how which* extant domestic institutions mediate between internationalization and national policy change, exploring, first, 'socioeconomic' (corporatism vs. pluralism) and, second, 'formal public' (constitutional setting) ones.[1] They argue that these influence the manner in which the adaptation unfolds because actual policy outcomes tend to *differ* from the mere change in societal preferences that were the immediate result of internationalization.

Their model will serve as the template for the present study but, in order to adopt it appropriately for the comparison between Germany and Canada, three aspects warrant close scrutiny. First, the authors take the way in which domestic interests change in response to economic globalization as given. While these propositions are well established (Frieden, 1991; Frieden and Rogowski, 1996), the literature on macro-regional integration implies that cross-country differences in how exactly similar dominant societal preferences manifest themselves might account for national variations in policy change (Cowles, 1995; Mayer, 1998).

Second, the key factor among Garrett and Lange's formal public institutions for the present study is the concept of institutional 'veto players' (Tsebelis, 1995). It is based on the premise that governmental actors legitimized through different constituencies will exhibit distinct interests in their dealings with each other. Employing the concept generally presumes clarity about the separation of powers among levels of government engrained in constitutional texts; this, however, increasingly may be compromised when governments sign international economic treaties. Third, in the specific context of this study, utilizing institutional VPs also depends upon definitional precision in what qualifies as 'federalism'; such analytical accuracy is less straightforward than is commonly believed (Duchacek, 1970).

The first section reviews the theoretical argument of Garrett and Lange (1996) regarding the institutions able to mediate between the societal preferences resulting from internationalization and the policy as well as institutional changes adopted by governments. The model's direct implications for the comparison between the German and Canadian federations are discussed. Sections 2 and 3 are devoted to exploring in more detail two tenets of Garrett and Lange's model, namely the way the interests of domestic actors line up in response to economic globalization, and the veto player theory. The fourth section deals with defining the crucial concept of federalism, before I formulate the analytical framework of this book in section 5.

Theorizing the Influence of Domestic Institutions

Garrett and Lange's Model

The authors devise the first analytical framework to date for explicating the causal manner in which extant domestic institutions intervene in how the adaptation process to globalization in different countries takes shape (see Figure 3.1).[2] Their model has four stages: the first one (1) develops predictions about how economic globalization influences the interests of domestic actors and their relative power *vis-à-vis* each other. The general proposition is that with an economy increasingly subject to international competition the number of actors that benefit increases, whereas the quantity of those that demand protection from foreign competition decreases.[3] Assuming that altered domestic interests *directly* result in an 'appropriate' change in government policy, that is, a dismantling of the Keynesian welfare state in favor of a deregulatory stance, this is the position of 'economic pluralism' (1996: 49).[4] Garrett and Lange take this proposition as given but hold that frequently the actual policy change *differs* from what economic pluralism would lead us to expect.[5] They maintain that this discrepancy can only be explained through the mediating role of domestic institutions between revised societal preferences induced by economic globalization and the government's reaction. Hence, economic pluralism is the null hypothesis of their framework.

The authors identify two sets of institutions. Stage II (2) represents *socioeconomic* institutions which affect the political clout of actors in the private sector distinguishes between three degrees of centralization in the labor market. In the first case, unions encompass only a small fraction of the entire labor force and their bargaining takes place primarily at the individual plant level. Canada and the United States are examples of these weak and decentralized unions. The second possibility is that individual unions exhibit a lot of power, but their joint organization on the national level is non-existent; Belgium and Italy fall into this category. Finally, a high level of unionization can be combined with either a unitary labor confederation and/or a single union as wage leader for all sectors of the economy. Austria is an example of the former, Germany of both.

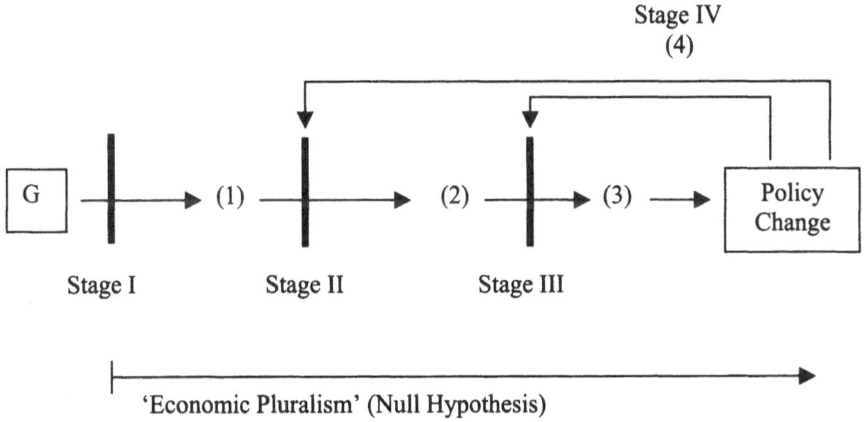

Figure 3.1 Garrett and Lange's Model

Source: adapted from Garrett and Lange (1996: 51)

Garrett and Lange point out that the difference between the 'extreme' cases of weak and decentralized unions on the one hand, and strong and centralized ones on the other, is negligible, since both allow reaping the benefits of the increase in tradable goods and services under internationalization (1996: 57).[6] Put differently, weak and decentralized unions result in a rather close adherence to the preferences in the now more important tradable sectors, whereas union confederations have the dual purpose of maintaining the external competitiveness of the tradable sectors and fostering solidarity among workers in the entire economy. Since they want to avoid wage increases in the non-tradable sectors that have the potential of instigating job losses in the export industries, the outcome is similar to the one under weak and decentralized unions (Garrett and Lange, 1996: 60).[7]

Stage III (3) in the causal chain signifies *formal public* institutions, which determine how governments respond to the tension between distributional demands emanating from the private sector (as filtered through socioeconomic institutions), and the macroeconomic constraints faced by governments under globalization. Formal public institutions, according to the authors (1996: 60–68), can have four different effects, the first two of which relate to the access of societal preferences to policy-making, whereas the latter two focus on the response by governments. The *regime type* juxtaposes (liberal) democracies and non-democracies, while among the former *electoral formulae* indicate the degree of bias toward certain domestic preferences over others in the voting procedure. As for the responsiveness of governments, the number of institutional *veto players*, that is, the actors whose agreement is required for policy change, as well as the extent of *bureaucratic autonomy* are considered to be the important factors.

Finally, Stage IV (4) investigates the conditions for endogenous change, namely whether or not the policy change adopted at the end of the third stage will result in a feedback loop, leading to subsequent alterations of the socioeconomic and/or formal public institutions themselves. Governments, whose first and foremost intention is to stay in power, may have incentives to alter the institutional structure of their polities to mitigate the tension between Keynesian demands for redistribution and economic performance. These changes are costly in the short term, for they are likely to harm the interests of the government's constituencies (1996: 69–72). Hence, the prospects for endogenous change depend on certain conditions, among them the degree of government risk aversion; the time until the next election; and the state of the international economy.

Garrett and Lange (1996: 75) emphasize that, although these five factors are likely to influence each other, for theory building it is important to first examine each of them separately. How this can be accomplished in the comparison between Germany and Canada is the topic of the next subsection.

Isolating Veto Players

As for the private interests mediated through the *socioeconomic* institutions, trade unions in Germany are structured in a very hierarchical fashion under the roof of the DGB (German Trade Union Association). Wage bargaining takes place in a certain sector and geographical area of the country, with the agreement subsequently being adopted by other sectors and regions with only minor alterations. By all accounts, Germany fulfils the criterion of having strong and centralized unions. Conversely, virtually the opposite holds true for Canada, for unions have no centralized control over representation, neither within nor across sectoral or geographical lines. Since strong, centralized and weak, decentralized labor market institutions exhibit very similar chances for reaping the benefits of internationalization in the tradable sectors, this aspect has no influence on the empirical comparison of this study; following Garrett and Lange, Stage II consequently can be excluded from further examination.

In terms of *formal public* institutions, the distinction between liberal democracies and non-democracies is of course irrelevant here. The second factor, the influence of electoral formulae on interest aggregation, requires closer scrutiny. Garrett and Lange, for analytical purposes, assume a two-sector economy (tradables versus non-tradables) and voters casting ballots solely on the basis of belonging to either one of the two sectors. They then distinguish four ways in which votes can be translated into seats: first, list proportional representation, used in most western European countries, results in an almost perfect conversion. Second, plurality vote in single member districts (like in the UK and Canada) leads to a similar outcome as under the first option, *if* tradable and non-tradable sectors are geographically concentrated. Third, seats can be apportioned according to political divisions (as in the US Senate) rather than population size. Finally, in a first-past-the post system where the two sectors are *not* geographically concentrated, one party will win *all* the votes (Garrett and Lange, 1996: 63–6).

In *all* electoral systems representation is based on the numerical strength of groups sharing a common concern, not on their economic power. In this sense, all electoral formulae 'distort' socioeconomic interests (the least in the first two systems, the most in the fourth one) but the point for the present investigation is that the German and Canadian voting procedures foster similar consequences. Germany has a mixed system in which half the Members of Parliament (MPs) are elected in single member districts, while the other half and the overall composition of the lower chamber, the Bundestag, is determined through proportional representation. Canada, on the other hand, consists of a clear first-past-the-post system in which all MPs are chosen in single member districts – with industries favoring protection versus those wishing to enhance liberalization being geographically concentrated. In addition, both countries have parliamentary systems (and incidentally the same number of political parties represented – five) with strict party discipline. Hence, the contrast between the traditional two-party coalitions in Germany and the Canadian one-party governments exhibits no significant consequences and the distinction in electoral formulae can be neglected.

The third component, the number of formal veto players required for domestic decision making, is based on the assumption that the interests of governmental actors differ to the extent that they accumulate interests in dissimilar ways. For instance, since national and constituent governments in a federation rely on geographically different electorates for legitimacy, the policies they pursue will reflect these distinctly aggregated mandates in the dealings between the two levels of government. This is the crucial aspect for the present analysis; both Germany and Canada are federal states, that is, both have constitutionally guaranteed veto players, yet the ways in which the respective constitutions regulate the means of exercising their veto power are quite different. This variation is captured in the popular notions of German 'cooperative' and Canadian 'competitive' federalism.[8] Garrett and Lange (1996: 66) maintain that the *number* of formal veto players determines the *speed* of adaptation; the more centralized the political system is, i.e. the fewer veto players it has, the faster the adjustment process.[9]

Finally, the authors criticize the literature on the fourth component of formal public institutions, the degree of bureaucratic independence from policy makers, for the 'lack of clarity about causal mechanisms and a paucity of rigorous empirical tests' (1996: 67). They consider work on the independence of central banks the only exception to this assessment. Both the German Bundesbank – now also the European Central Bank – and the Bank of Canada are constitutionally free from government interference. In sum, three of the four factors under formal public institutions are either constant or negligible; thus, Stage III can be limited to the influence of formal veto players.

Yet, three features of Garrett and Lange's causal model require clarification for the present study. These relate to, first, whether the propositions about the change of domestic actors' preferences (Stage I) are so universal that they indeed can be taken as given. Second, I examine whether the veto player concept (Stage III) is able to capture the existing variation among federal constitutions; and third, how 'federalism' is to be operationalized in a way that allows us to actually utilize the veto player concept. I will discuss these aspects in turn in the following three sections.

Explaining Variation among Regional Governance Structures

Garrett and Lange take the propositions about how domestic actors alter their interests and the relative power of these groups in relation to each other in consequence of economic globalization as given. Frieden and Rogowski (1996) had established that the strength of domestic actors favoring to reduce provisions of the Keynesian welfare state increases with international competition; these are groups that expect to benefit from domestic deregulation, as they are engaged in the tradables sectors. While the authors maintain that their prediction holds *universally* in countries being affected by economic globalization in a similar fashion, some doubt might be cast on this view. Mattli (1999) had argued that pressure from business in both the EU and NAFTA was instrumental in bringing about these two 'successful' macro-regions (cf. Chapter 2), the interests and goals pursued by the respective economic actors in fact varied considerably. The latter were also faced with opposition to the noted integration schemes to varying degrees.

In the Europe, the ERT's purpose was to press for a Community-wide standardization of rules and regulations governing market exchange; for achieving this goal, the Roundtable opposed a mere deregulation of national standards. 'In the eyes of the French members [representing the largest group], the ERT was a "Christian Democratic/Social Democratic group" that did not share the ideology of the Thatcherite capitalists' and was not subscribing to the Anglo-Saxon idea of mere lobbying but rather to the development of concrete proposals (Cowles, 1995: 512). For instance, ERT members developed several transborder infrastructure proposals, designed to link the UK and the Scandinavian countries with the European continent (Cowles, 1995: 505–9).

The businesses advocating the SEA brought forth their policy proposals and, together with the EC executive, the Commission, drafted the ultimate agreement and worked toward persuading the governments of the member states to ratify it. By contrast, the trade unions did not involve themselves in this process at all (Sandholtz and Zysman, 1989: 97). Being, like the Commission, in favor of Community-wide labor regulations, national unions as well as the ETUC (the European Trade Union Confederation) have not opposed the SEA. Instead, ETUC and UNICE (the Union of Industrial and Employers' Confederations of Europe) agreed on collective negotiations with the Commission over the EU social and employment directives associated with the SEA.

In comparison, the trilateral NAFTA negotiations, like the previous CUSFTA talks, were divided into 19 working groups. The US and Canadian negotiators each had to consult with 30 advisory committees from the private sector, pressing for specific phase-outs, rules of origins or exemptions for particular industries, ranging from the banking sector to the automotive industry to agricultural producers. When the negotiations were completed in August 1992 at the height of the US presidential election campaign, Bill Clinton, as eventual successor to then President George Bush, positioned himself as willing to conclude the NAFTA only if separate agreements on labor and the environment were negotiated.[10] In this process, the opposition grew larger and its ideological spectrum broader than during the initial fast track campaign. It now included the unions and the so-called Citizen's Trade Campaign, which rose to 'three hundred environmental, community, human rights, and other grassroots organizations claiming membership of more than five million members' (Mayer, 1998:295), but also Ross Perot and the political Right under Republican Pat Buchanan.[11]

After members of Congress had come under intense pressure over the summer in their constituencies to oppose NAFTA ratification, an unprecedented marketing and lobbying campaign by the business community was launched, forcing its members to momentarily set aside the specific interests they were fighting for during the trade negotiations. Together with the President and mainstream environmental groups, they eventually won congressional approval for NAFTA in November 1993.[12]

Given these marked differences, what accounts for the institutional variations of successful integration schemes? The sociological concept of 'morphogenetic cycles' offers an explanation for this variation.

Culture Penetrating Structure: The Concept of Morphogenetic Cycles

While the relationship between structure and agency has been widely discussed in social theory, this cannot be said for the connection between culture and agency. Against this backdrop, Archer proposes a transfer of the conceptual apparatus developed in the agent-structure debate to the cultural realm.[13] Since social life can be considered as the 'interplay between interests and ideas' (1996: xi), subsuming both structural and cultural analyses under the same conceptual umbrella allows for an examination of the interplay between them. In order to develop this unified framework, she advances five analytical points.[14]

First, most approaches within the agent-structure debate suffer from either one of three logically possible forms of conflation, that is, of treating one or even both categories as not open to investigation. Downwards conflation views agent behavior as dominated by an externally given structure, whereas upwards conflation stresses the importance of actors in social life. Central conflation asserts mutual constitution and thereby does not permit the disentanglement of structure and agency for empirical analysis.[15] Second and subsequently, although structure is intertwined with agency, Archer maintains that the two nonetheless must be kept *analytically* distinct, for the interplay between them over time is impossible to investigate otherwise.

Third, in order to model this interrelation, it is essential to begin the analysis with the pre-existing context that constrains present actors when shaping the structural system within which future actors will find themselves. Fourth, this interplay between structure and agency can be analyzed through so-called morphogenetic cycles.

> As a process 'morphogenesis' refers to the complex interchanges that produce change in a System's given form, structure or state ('morphostasis' is the reverse), the end-product being termed 'Elaboration'. Of course action is ceaseless and essential to both the stable continuum and further elaboration of the system. However, when morphogenesis results, then subsequent interaction will be different from earlier action precisely because it is now conditioned by the elaborate consequences of that earlier action. Hence the morphogenetic perspective is not only dualistic but also sequential, dealing in endless three-part cycles of Structural Conditioning → Social interaction → Structural Elaboration (Archer, 1996: xxiv).

Fifth, by transferring this approach to the cultural field, both structural and cultural realms can be conceptualized as parallel, relatively autonomous, morphogenetic cycles, and the interplay between interests and ideas can be explored. Structure and culture intersect in the middle segment, that is, the agent-level, of their respective cycles in one of two possible ways: either a cultural penetration of structure or vice versa. In the context of the present discussion, only the former variant is of relevance. Archer asserts that cultural factors influence the structural field when a material interest group endorses 'any doctrine (theory, belief or ideology) for the advancement of those interests (that is their articulation, assertion, or legitimation)' (1996: 284). While conflicting material interest groups associate themselves with opposing ideologies, this nevertheless permits the possibility that the open manifestation of contrasting interests will *not* ensue.

> ... it needs be allowed that the discursive success of one set of ideas helps to account for the victory of the group advancing it, when structural factors alone (such as bargaining power, numbers, or organization) fail to provide an explanation. Similarly, cultural factors often have to be deemed accountable for the *failure of conflict to manifest itself* although the structural conditions appear ripe. ... social groups not only have interests, resources and power but they also have ideas ... (Archer, 1996: 283–4; my emphasis).

In sum, Archer's thesis is twofold: first, the structural and cultural fields, although conceptually distinct, are interconnected through the actors being part of both realms simultaneously; it is here where culture penetrates structure. Second, cultural factors are considered responsible for either promoting or preventing conflict between material interest groups. The question then remains how 'culture' thus defined can be operationalized; the approach most common in the literature would suggest a rethinking of the corporatist/pluralist partition in Stage II.

Operationalizing 'Culture': Corporatism versus Pluralism

The cultural impact can be operationalized as the difference between the continental European (and Scandinavian) corporatist versus the North American pluralist view concerning the role of 'the state' in 'the market'. The separation focuses on the relative importance of what Fiscal Federalism conceptualizes as the distribution function of the public sector, that is, individual and/or collective income redistribution. By framing the corporatist/pluralist distinction in this manner, it coincides with different welfare state (WS) models.[16] A number of studies support the view that it is reasonable to differentiate between the continental European and North American countries in this way (Zeigler, 1988; Esping-Andersen, 1990). Although the forms of corporatism within the EU and to a lesser extent of pluralism within the NAFTA vary in degree, the corporatist/pluralist distinction is one of a kind.[17] Corporatist governance structures are marked by a comparatively stronger regulatory and distributive state involvement in the economy than is the case in a pluralist regime. Thus the respective modes of social organization lead to differing propositions about the process of conflict resolution and subsequently about the institutional outcome. The argument here is that political-institutional differences in the regulation of market forces on the international level are influenced by the prevalent 'culture' of state intervention in the domestic economy.

The normative roots of *corporatism* are to be found in collectivism, which assumes the existence of a common good. Since the source of conflict is inequality, however the latter term is understood in a given society, the mode of conflict resolution that corporatism seeks is containment; in other words, conflict is seen as pathological, since it inevitably inhibits the achievement of the common good. *Pluralism*, on the other hand, is normatively founded on individualism, marked by the pursuit of self-interest by citizens who in turn make up society. It follows that no concept of a common good exists independently of what is determined through the mechanism of supply and demand in the market place. Therefore, conflict is viewed, at a minimum, as unavoidable but generally as positive. The function of politics in this environment is to manage conflicts by instituting rules according to which disputes between competing interests can be settled.

Given their respective normative assumptions, both corporatism and pluralism display distinct procedural features regarding the interrelation between *actors* and consequently lead one to expect varied institutional *outcomes*. In a corporatist setting, in order to contain conflict, a limited number of top organizations, usually business and labor, are incorporated by the government (hence the term 'corporatism') into the public policy making process through close consultation.[18] This involvement is *active*, meaning the two societal groups contribute to the development of public policy with their own proposals; in addition, despite naturally divergent economic interests, it is also ultimately *consensual*. Business and labor are not fragmented into sector-specific interests but are structured centrally and hierarchically; they are thus able to credibly represent their views in corporatist negotiations. The public policy outcomes under corporatism tend to exhibit clear institutional arrangements ('big government') with social regulations of market actors as well as social policy.[19] As Zeigler notes, 'implementation of an incomes policy is a fundamental criterion of the definition of societal corporatism'.[20]

Pluralism, by contrast, does not procedurally limit the number of interest groups that can seek access to political decision-makers, with the strength of an interest group seen as depending on its stake in a particular issue area. These groups, like individuals in pluralist understanding, represent their narrowly defined interests by way of *lobbying*; they do not engage with government in the development of concrete policies. The institutional outcome is likely to involve limited regulation, since an essential feature of individualism is the rejection of government interference beyond the functions of a 'night watchman state'; hence, a close connection exists between pluralism and neoliberal market ideology. Given this, some authors have elevated the corporatist/pluralist distinction, originally developed to denote varied national models, in the mid-1980s to the macro-regional level, conceptualizing continental European *neo*corporatism and North American *neoliberalism* as different modes of social organization instead (for example, Stubbs, 1998).[21]

I want to clarify one conceptual aspect before proceeding. The argument here is *not* that European institutions differ from North American institutions because they exhibit distinct 'cultures' of the state's involvement in the market, and that we know that they have different 'cultures' because the institutions are different; this would be tautological. Instead, the variance in PTA institutions is explained by 'cultural' similarities among the *member states* that comprise a given macro-region. *This* stylized correspondence makes it likely that member states with a higher degree of state involvement in the 'market', pool sovereignty at the PTA level to a higher degree, whereas the opposite holds for the institutional depth of a macro-region between member states with a relatively lower political involvement in the economy.

Since the neocorporatist/pluralist distinction, that is, the influence of 'culture' on the concrete manner in which domestic actors voice their material preferences resembles what Garrett and Lange advanced as the organization of the labor market as the crucial component of 'socioeconomic institutions', Stage II can still be held constant. This does not negate the fact that European and US business interests (due to a different 'culture') diverged on the type of economic integration they pressured for, or that the opposition to the PTA preferred by business was consequently heavily opposed only in the NAFTA case. However, this would be analytically relevant only *if* this had a demonstrable effect on the operation of institutional VPs (that is, the constitutional setup); this is implausible and the impact of Stage II continues to be negligible. Hence, the concept of institutional veto players in Stage III remains the factor isolated for the empirical comparison of this study; it is to this notion that we now turn.

Conceptualizing Veto Players

Tsebelis' Argument

While Garrett and Lange (1996: 66) mention the concept of formal veto players in the specific context of their own framework, Tsebelis (1995) invented it for a far broader purpose. His intention is to compare political systems across regime types (parliamentarism versus presidentialism), as well as party (two- and multi-party) and legislature (unicameral versus bicameral) arrangements under a single theoretical umbrella. The dependent variable in this endeavor is the *potential* for policy change, that is, the chance for altering the status quo across varied institutional settings; quelling policy change is labeled as 'stability'. Tsebelis operationalizes policy stability in a formal manner as the 'size of the winset of the status quo' (1995: 295), meaning the areas of agreement among different actors (for example, parties in parliament) to *defeat* the status quo. It follows that the smaller the winset of the *status quo*, the smaller are the chances of enacting significant (rather than, if at all, piecemeal) policy change.[22]

The veto player argument enters the analysis as the explanatory variable. Generally, veto players are defined as actors whose agreement is required for a policy decision. Concretely, this means that VPs only qualify as such if they can effectively *block* a policy change from being adopted. Tsebelis identifies two primary categories of VPs, namely institutional and partisan ones (1995: 302).[23] While institutional VPs are explicitly identified in the constitution, the latter depend on a country's specific party and government system. Hence, the agreement of institutional VPs to a proposed policy change is both necessary and sufficient. By contrast, the consent of partisan VPs, that is, the political parties in a coalition government, might be neither necessary nor sufficient to alter the *status quo*. If coalition partners were bypassed through a minority government, their agreement would no longer be a necessity. Should the coalition partners lack the power to prevent their own MPs from voting against a government proposal in parliament, agreement in the coalition would not be sufficient (Tsebelis, 1995: 302–3). The conceptual link between the dependent and independent variables is that:

> [...] the policy stability of a political system depends on three characteristics of its veto players: their number, their congruence (the difference in their political positions) and their cohesion (the similarity of policy positions of the constituent units of each veto player) (Tsebelis, 1995: 301).

Generally, the higher the *number* of VPs, the higher is the likelihood of maintaining the *status quo* (policy stability); in other words, the lower is the potential for policy change. In terms of institutional VPs, they are only considered as such if two criteria are fulfilled: their legitimacy has to be based on differently sized constituencies, since this will lead to varied interests between them. Further, they must have *formal* veto power. This means that bicameral legislatures do not necessarily and always exhibit more than one VP, since, first, bicameral systems are not necessarily also federal ones. In unitary states, upper and lower houses are either both elected in national constituencies, in which case they are identical, as in the Netherlands, Italy and France; or the upper chamber is not elected but appointed, as in the United Kingdom. Second, even in some federations, members of the upper house are appointed rather than elected, as in Canada. Against this backdrop, Tsebelis maintains that the only cases in which upper chambers still have formal veto power are federations like the USA, Germany and Switzerland (1995: 310). Yet, even here, irrespective of whether being elected directly (as the Senators in the United States) or indirectly (as the members of the German Bundesrat), the upper chamber's consent is not required for *all* legislation, meaning that it does not have formal veto power in every instance.[24]

Therefore, to determine the exact number of VPs, their *congruence* becomes important. The basic argument is that the winset of the *status quo* increases (the potential for policy change decreases), the bigger the distance between VPs; hence, the bigger the distance, the lower is the congruence among them. Concretely, this means that the number of institutional actors can be higher than the number of formal VPs. This can occur in two situations: first, if their composition is identical, that is, they represent the same – namely a national – electorate; second, if the two chambers are legitimized by different constituencies but the upper house cannot block legislation at all or at least not in all cases. In either of these instances, the *absorption rule* applies which means that the two institutional actors are counted as one VP. By contrast, political parties are always to be counted as separate VPs, since they will stress their ideological differences to voters, even if they were to agree on a number of positions. In other words, the absorption rule *only* applies to institutional actors (in case of congruence between the two houses) but *never* to partisan actors, i.e. the number of parties in a coalition government.

The third independent variable influencing the potential for policy change is the *cohesion* of each VP. A political party with small ideological differences displays a high level of cohesion. However, a party with large divisions could nonetheless be similarly cohesive, if the MPs are grouped around the leadership in such a fashion that the party as a whole can behave coherently despite disagreements among its individuals.[25] As cohesion has relevance only for partisan VPs, it will not be discussed here any further.

The implication of these counting rules for the context of this study is that Germany ranges between two and three veto players, depending on whether the coalition that rules in the Bundestag (first chamber) simultaneously controls the Bundesrat (second chamber). Canada, on the other hand, has only one VP, namely the opposition to its single party governments in parliament; its upper house, the Senate, consists of prime ministerial appointees and it can delay but has no power to permanently block legislation introduced by parliament (Tsebelis, 1995: 318). Thus, given that the potential for policy change decreases with the number of VPs, we should expect that the governmental response, and thereby the institutional adaptation, to changing societal preferences due to internationalization must be swifter in Canada than in Germany.

What Lies Beneath: Institutional VPs beyond the Second Chamber

Such an assessment presents a puzzle, for, as will be demonstrated in Chapters 3 and 4, the realities of domestic adjustment in the two countries appear to indicate the opposite. The ratification of the Maastricht Treaty in Germany was more expeditious than the implementation of the NAFTA side agreements in Canada. To account for this supposed contradiction requires two clarifications and one amendment of the veto player concept. As for the former, trying to explain the variation among different federal countries in the ratification and/or implementation of regional integration treaties, themselves a consequence of internationalization, has two implications for the VPs considered in this study. First, partisan VPs can be excluded from the examination entirely, since the question of preserving their constitutionally guaranteed powers from encroachment through international treaties signed by the federal government combines constituent governments *regardless* of the different political parties ruling on the federal and subnational levels.[26] Second, for my purposes the absorption rule does *not* apply to the German Bundesrat because the second chamber constitutionally *is* a veto player in the domestic ratification process of international treaties that affect Länder competencies.

Beyond these clarifications, the number of VPs in Canada requires further scrutiny. According to Money and Tsebelis (1992), Canada does *not* have any institutional VPs, since its upper chamber, the Senate, is not legitimized by differently sized constituencies (because the members are appointed by the prime minister), and it does not have the formal power to block policies introduced by parliament. None the less, Canada *does* indeed possess institutional veto players, namely the ten provincial governments. Their Premiers meet on a regular basis (usually every six months) with the Canadian Prime Minister in what have become known as First Ministers' Conferences. However, this forum for domestic intergovernmental relations is not officially mentioned in the constitution but rather is common practice, complemented by meetings of senior officials on specific issues in the interim. In this sense, limiting institutional veto players to upper chambers and the role assigned to them according to the formal constitution can be misleading. The counting of VPs would have to be broadened to include not only the formal but also the *informal* aspects of constitutional settings.[27]

Conceptualizing institutional VPs in this way is based on the premise that constitutional rules in general, and among federations in particular, are unambiguous. The next section will probe into this assumption.

Murky Waters: Defining Federalism

The constitutional separation between unitary and federal systems is the most inclusive and common one, either explicitly or, since much of the literature deals with federations *only*, at least implicitly. While many of the early studies have been rather legalistic (for instance, Wheare, 1953; McWhinney, 1962), more recent ones, particularly in the European context, also appeared to be concerned with *promoting* federalism as a constitutional setup for the EU (Burgess and Gagnon, 1993). Others focused on the interrelationship with capitalism (Hueglin, 1990), challenging the early notion by Harold Laski (1939) that federalism will be increasingly eroded by the forces of capitalism and hence become an obsolescent form of government. In this vein, a lot of attention has recently been given to examining whether specific federations were constitutionally prepared to adjust to changes in the global economy (Brown and Smith, 1991; Boothe, 1996). Yet, Duchacek (1970) has cast some doubt on the analytical usefulness of the dichotomy between federal and unitary states. He observed that:

> Federalism has now become one of those good echo words that evoke a positive response but that may mean all things to all men, like *democracy*, *socialism*, *progress*, *constitution*, *justice*, or *peace*. We see the term applied to almost any successful combination of unity with diversity, to almost any form of pluralism and cooperation within and among nations (Duchacek, 1970: 191; emphasis in original).

He none the less discerns from the literature on federalism one feature common to all studies and develops it into a tentative working definition, namely that a federal system exhibits a constitutional division of power between one general and several subnational governments (1970: 194). He subjects this definition to exploring the term 'federal' in the constitutional texts of those countries that are, or claim to be, federal.[28] To do so, on the basis of the American federation he determines 'ten yardsticks', which are seen as crucial features of a federal system, and investigates the degree to which they apply in the countries under consideration.[29]

The ten yardsticks explore the following aspects: 1) the extent to which the central government has exclusive control over foreign relations; 2) whether or not the federation is constitutionally immune against secession; 3) whether or not the central government display a sphere of domestic authority that is independent of the approval by the constituent units; 4) whether the central government or the component units have the ultimate say over changes to the federal constitution; 5) whether or not the autonomy of subnational governments can be eliminated; 6) which of the two levels of government is allocated the significant, and which one the residual powers; 7) the nature of bicameralism, i.e. the extent to which unequal units are represented equally in the upper house; 8) whether or not independent courts exist for the national and the subnational level; 9) the role of the supreme court in interpreting the constitution; 10) the extent to which a clear division of powers is guaranteed by the constitution.

Duchacek's assessment of these yardsticks against the constitutions of 21 countries that at the time of his writing either were, or claimed to be, federations, warranted two important findings. First, the individual yardsticks do not have equal weight in determining whether or not a country qualifies as federal. For instance, the relevance of having independent court systems at the national and subnational levels is a minor criterion, whereas a clear division of powers between the central government and the component units is considered as far more crucial. Yet, this does not mean that the yardsticks provide guidance in settling whether the absence of one aspect can be compensated for by the presence of others. Put differently, the application of the ten yardsticks still does not provide an unequivocal finding on what constitutes a federal system (Duchacek, 1970: 273–4).

The second, and closely related, inference is that the distinction between centralized and federal systems is not as clear-cut as is commonly believed. The tenth yardstick, the clear division of powers between national and subnational levels of government and therefore the supposed 'core' of all federal definitions, is particularly instructive in this regard. In virtually no federation does a clear domestic separation of powers exist. 'Here, again, we observe how federal constitutions point to a dilemma rather than an unequivocal solution' (Duchacek, 1970: 259).[30]

On the other hand, unitary states exhibit a division of competencies between national and subnational governments as well. While unitary decentralization *de jure* differs from federal arrangements in so far as the territorial distribution of authority is exercised through delegation from the central authority and hence can theoretically be revoked or redistributed at any point without consent from the affected units, this *de facto* is an unlikely case. The grant of territorial self-rule is mostly considered as practically, although not constitutionally, irrevocable (Duchacek, 1970: 352).

In addition, the centralizing tendencies among federations have also prompted a conceptual blurring among centralized and federal systems (Duchacek, 1970: 348). These findings would seem to confirm his central proposition that, while federalism is primarily about the territorial dimension of politics, so are all forms of government, be they federal or unitary, liberal-democratic or authoritarian. In one way or another, it is imperative for them, if only for reasons of administrative efficiency, to organize polities along territorial lines (Duchacek, 1970: 4).

However, it appears that his findings are in part due to the wide variety of federal systems he explored. They ranged from the 'classical' federations (the United States, Canada, Australia, Germany and Switzerland) to more unstable examples (Nigeria, Malaysia and the former Yugoslavia) to what were *de facto* centralized countries (like the former Soviet Union). By including countries in his study that merely *claim* to be federal, Duchacek's judgment is perhaps inevitable. The analytical distinction between centralized and federal systems appears to hold if the number of countries is limited to the standard federations of the OECD world. Bakvis and Chandler (1987a: 4) claim it is still reasonable to hold that '[w]hat continues to distinguish federal from so-called unitary states is the degree to which relationships are formalized and shaped through constitutional means'. This suggests that, contra Duchacek, it *does* matter whether the competencies of subnational units, whatever their extent, are constitutionally guaranteed or not.[31] While the devolution of powers in unitary systems indeed may practically be difficult to revoke at a later date, realignment of competencies by the center is nonetheless possible in a notably easier fashion, that is, without adjustment of constitutional provisions.

Even if this was accepted, the literature on federalism, and Duchacek is no exception here, is chiefly concerned with domestic issues. An unambiguous separation of powers in individual federations between the two levels of government may persist as long as matters of intrastate relevance are at issue; it is likely to lose clarity, however, with the 'intrusion' of international politics in the domestic realm. Specifically international economic treaties have the potential to compromise the internal 'balance of powers', to the extent that it has not been altered in the meantime already, because of different functions. The reason which is most relevant for the current study has to do with the federal monopoly in foreign relations and the possible spillover resulting from it. The conclusion of international treaties by the national executive can infringe on competencies that domestically fall under the jurisdiction of the component units. If the latter have the right to prevent the implementation of such treaties, the federal government can no longer exert credible commitments on the international scene for the country as a whole and may instead become a victim to particularistic interests at home. Conversely, if subnational governments have no leverage in these circumstances, their exclusive powers become at best concurrent, if not meaningless. The national government might 'sign away' competencies to a supranational body that domestically fall under subnational jurisdiction. The extent to which this causes subsequent difficulties with the ratification and/or implementation process in different federations exhibits an even clearer federal/unitary distinction than is the case in 'merely' domestic politics.

Since *all* competencies in unitary systems constitutionally rest with the central government, regardless of any decentralization, the powers of subnational governments can*not* be compromised through the signing of international treaties. Precisely this, however, necessarily instigates constitutional debates in federal systems. Gibbins (1987) holds that federal systems, once established, are able to maintain their own survival, even if the underlying societal and/or economic reasons that originally gave rise to their formation change. He attributes this persistence of federations exactly to the ability of constituent units to defend their competencies on constitutional grounds. Thus, adjustments take place mostly at the informal rather than the formal level of constitutional change. Chapters 4 and 5 will attempt to determine the extent to which this proposition is generalizable across different federal systems.

Drawing again on Duchacek's yardsticks, the discussion of different federations can be broken down into three, albeit closely related, aspects. First, the formal division of powers between the federal and subnational governments determines the *range* of issues that can potentially be contentious between the center and the constituent units. Second, the bicameral arrangements, that is, the way in which the component units are represented in the second chamber of parliament and which powers this institution has, indicate the *form* that the interaction might take. Finally, the combination of the first two aspects leads to a certain *kind* of intergovernmental relations.

Having examined in detail three features of Garrett and Lange's model and how they affect the comparison between the German and Canadian federations, the analytical framework of this study can now be developed.

Synthesis: The Analytical Framework

The different elements contained in Figure 3.2 are conceptualized in the following manner. A change in international economic conditions, for short Globalization (G), causes an alteration in the interests of domestic actors and the relative power *vis-à-vis* each other in Stage I (1). This shift will lead to a strengthening of domestic actors that favor a dismantling of the Keynesian welfare state, whereas the influence of groups expecting to lose from

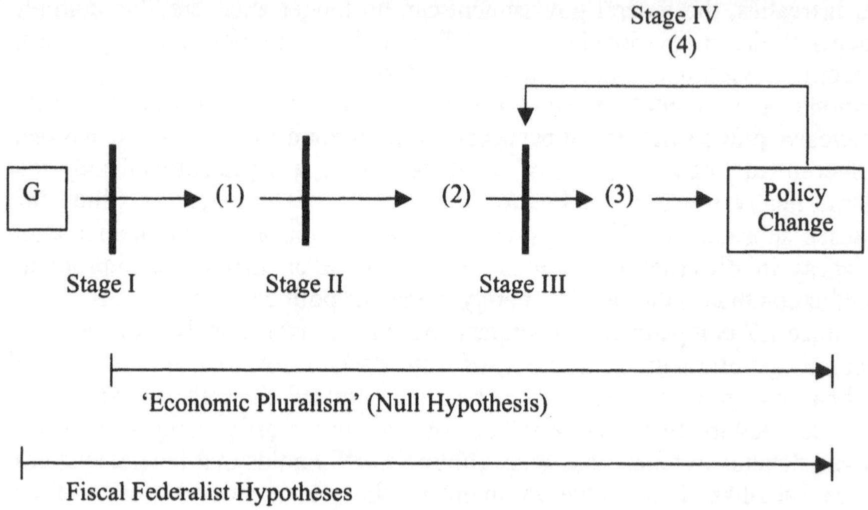

Figure 3.2 Analytical Framework

increased foreign competition and demand protection is in decline. This conforms to Garrett and Lange's approach; Stage I is the antecedent condition of this study, that is, its very presence (and its extent) sets the causal mechanism in motion (cf. King *et al.*, 1994; Van Evera, 1997).

Somewhat in contrast to the proposition of Frieden and Rogowski (1996), Mattli (1999) had demonstrated that reaping the benefits of a more open, deregulated economy by its proponents depends upon open markets of the main trading partners and the free access to those markets. In other words, parallel to favoring domestic policy change, it necessitates the simultaneous promotion of international treaties by the business community to secure this access and promote common regulations. However, economic actors in the EU and the NAFTA had promoted quite different strategies and goals. I have suggested that this variation could be captured through the sociological concept of morphogenetic cycles (Archer, 1996), claiming that 'culture' can explain differences among domestic groups with the same material interests.

Two, albeit closely related, ways of operationalizing the concept of 'culture' are to distinguish between neocorporatist and pluralist interest aggregation or, alternatively, between different forms of capitalism in Germany and Canada. Either one approximates the organization of the labor market as the incarnation of Garrett and Lange's 'socioeconomic institutions'. The authors' proposition is that the extremes of strong, centralized and weak, decentralized labor market institutions foster the *same* outcome with regard to economic actors capitalizing on the opportunities presented by internationalization. Thus, the impact of Stage II (2) is, at best, negligible.

Stage III (3) denotes the formal public institutions. I have argued that three of them (democracy/non-democracy, electoral formulae and bureaucratic autonomy) can be held constant as well, so that the role of institutional veto players is isolated for discussion in this study. Yet, the treatment of Tsebelis (1995) has presented a puzzle in its consequences especially for the Canadian case. Therefore, I include here constitutional aspects that are *informal* in the sense that they do not necessarily relate to the role of the second chamber (on which Tsebelis concentrates) but directly to subnational governments. The number of (formal and informal) institutional veto players is the *independent* variable of Stage III.

The international economic treaties concluded by the two national governments represent the *policy change* in our analysis. In other words, contrary to Garrett and Lange's model the policy change is not domestic *per se*, but the domestic decision to supranationalize certain public sector functions. I will be examining treaties where the public sector functions in question formerly fell under subnational jurisdiction. The institutional variation among PTAs is the *dependent* variable of Stage III.

This will be manifest in the feedback loop of Stage IV (4). Again in contrast to Garrett and Lange, the feedback loop is dependent upon the same veto players as Stage III. The role of subnational governments in the conclusion of international economic treaties that potentially embark on their competencies can be twofold. First, they can attempt to influence the federal government during the negotiations of the treaty in question (Stage III). In both countries, consultation mechanisms have been established for this purpose. Second, component governments play a decisive role in the domestic ratification and/or implementation process (Stage IV).[32] The possible outcomes range from formal constitutional change to the *de facto* blocking of the ratification/implementation process. In the latter case, the constituent units would showcase the inability of the federal government to credibly commit to the international obligations it signed. Which of these outcomes is more likely in Stage IV depends, like Stage III, on the exact codification of subnational competencies in the constitution. Thus, in Stage IV the causal process is reverse. The regional integration scheme becomes the *independent* variable, whereas the (absence or presence) of constitutional change following the PTA's conclusion then is the *dependent* variable.

As for Garrett and Lange, *economic pluralism* is the study's null hypothesis. If it were confirmed, altered domestic interests would translate directly into the appropriate government change. The mediating influence of socioeconomic and formal public domestic institutions would be irrelevant. By contrast, the *fiscal federalist hypotheses* make their propositions starting from the implications of economic globalization directly, bypassing the role of changed domestic interests; like economic pluralism, they ignore the influence of extant domestic institutions.[33] The fiscal federalist propositions serve as the background of the current study.

Notes

1 Rockman (1994) points out that all institutionalist analyses, irrespective of their particular foci, agree that the architecture of institutions, their rules as well as the meanings embodied in their procedures are consequential. Pierson (2000) emphasizes the constraining factors that constitutional arrangements, which ultimately are designed to persist, pose for future options. Once established, their change becomes increasingly costly to policy makers over time, albeit not impossible. Gibbins (1987) holds that adjustments in federations largely take place at an *informal* rather than formal level of constitutional change.

2 Exploring the varied ways in which European economies adapt to globalization, Regini (2000: 8–9) agrees on the role of preexisting institutions as intervening between exogenous change and the domestic response to them. Institutional constraints and incentives, however, are not entirely deterministic.

3 Depending on the economic model being adopted, the groups primarily affected by internationalization, both positively and negatively, are aligned either on the basis of factors of production (Stolper-Samuelson theorem) or along sectoral lines (Ricardo-Viner approach).

4 This argument has been made both for trade (Frieden and Rogowski, 1996) and for international finance (Frieden, 1991).

5 Note that economic pluralism and the fiscal federalist hypotheses differ regarding the starting point of their respective propositions. The former focuses on the altered preferences of domestic actors as a result of economic globalization, whereas the latter makes inferences from internationalization directly.

6 This is so because wage setting in the tradable and non-tradable sectors display different rationales. While wages in the former are largely determined through competitiveness in world markets, unions in the latter can push for wage increases with less fear of fostering unemployment. However, stronger wage increases in non-tradable sectors can lead to inflationary pressures, higher interest rates to combat the former, subsequently an appreciated exchange rate as foreign investors take advantage of the higher interest rates, which then hurts the tradable sectors because their goods become more expensive in export markets.

7 The authors emphasize that the same argument can be made for the organization of employers in an economy; thus, by implication Stage II denotes countries with either pluralist or corporatist modes of conflict resolution as equal in outcome.

8 Alternatively, German 'intrastate' and Canadian 'interstate' federalism can be juxtaposed. The former marks national-level institutions (the Bundesrat) for the conduct of international relations, whereas the latter typifies provinces carrying out their distinct foreign policy in matters under their jurisdiction, not always coordinating with the federal government (Michelmann, 1986: 540–41).

9 This position implies that unitary states always adjust more swiftly than federations; it is corroborated by findings in Fiscal Federalism (Hülsemeyer, 2000). By contrast, Schmidt (1999) has charged that federations adapted more easily than unitary states to the challenges of the Maastricht Treaty. The concomitant loss of power by national executives to EU institutions was supposedly less problematic in the former because federal governments had a more restricted grip on domestic power than the latter to begin with.

10 The move was intended to distance himself from Bush senior without rejecting NAFTA altogether, while trying to satisfy enough Democrats sympathetic to labor and environmental interests to eventually win Congressional endorsement.

11 To illustrate the ideological diversity of the opposition, Buchanan suggested, 'let us take America back from the global parasites of the World Bank and the IMF, who siphon off America's wealth for Third World socialists and incompetents' (cited in Mayer, 1998: 232).

12 In short, contrary to the SEA experience, the NAFTA negotiations consisted of merely sectoral lobbying by the business 'community', an array of opposition groups that were divided along several ideological cleavage lines, as well as a mostly uncompromising 'debate' between advocates and opponents.

13 Archer readily concedes that the term 'culture' is riddled with descriptive and explanatory paucity 'What culture and what culture does are issues bogged down in a conceptual morass from which no adequate sociology of culture has been able to emerge' (1996: 2). For this reason, she deliberately 'travels light' (1996: xiii) and makes little to no reference to the major works in cultural studies; her scholarly concern is theorizing the intersection of ideas and material interests rather than a discussion of 'culture' itself. Thus, in the operationalization of the term for the purposes of this book (see below), I use it in quotation marks to clarify the absence of any conncetion with cultural studies. For an analytical overview of the latter, see Wilson (2000).

14 Carlsnaes (1992) has formalized her approach and transferred it to the field of foreign policy analysis.

15 Within the discipline of International Relations, prominent examples of the three fallacies of conflation are neorealism (Waltz, 1979), intergovernmentalism (Moravcsik, 1991) and structuration theory (Wendt, 1987), respectively.

16 Esping-Andersen (1990) distinguishes between the corporatist (Austria, France, Germany, Italy) and social-democratic (Norway, Sweden, Denmark) WS forms on the one hand, and the liberal version (USA, Canada, Australia) on the other, viewing them as three discrete regime clusters. In contrast, Rhodes (1998: 116–18) detects a gradual convergence within the EU on the German corporatist variant.

17 Siaroff (1999) suggests replacing the concept of corporatism, due to varied understandings of the term in the literature, with the ordinal measure of 'integration'. None the less, he confirms that even then OECD countries can be grouped into two clusters, which mostly coincide with the corporatist/pluralist divide.

18 The distinction between corporatism and pluralism, specifically regarding the degree of centralization of organized labor, closely resembles Garrett and Lange's socioeconomic institutions.

19 Social regulations set common standards of working conditions to avoid the threat of 'social dumping', while social policy refers to the redistributive means associated with the welfare state (see Majone, 1993).

20 Zeigler (1988: 70) distinguishes between 'societal corporatism' in Europe and 'state corporatism' in Latin America and Asia. Hence, the term is used here merely in the sense of its societal variant.

21 The differences between the two forms of capitalism on the domestic level are explored in Crouch and Streeck (1997). For their continued prevalence regarding the institutional distinction between various macro-regions, see Coleman and Underhill (1998). Also note that this conceptualization approximates Cerny's three forms of the competition state. Neocorporatism, depending on its degree, can resemble either the continental European or the traditional centralized versions, while neoliberalism is almost synonymous with the Anglo-American model of the competition state (cf. Chapter 2).

22 For the formalized argumentation, see Tsebelis (1995: 295–301).

23 He emphasizes that, depending on the concrete political system, additional VPs might have to be considered, for instance, the top organizations of employers and unions in corporatist systems. However, since these factors are rather idiosyncratic, he excludes them from consideration in his argument. For the purposes of the present study, they can also be neglected because the focus is on institutional VPs.

24 How exactly the power of second chambers plays out in cases where they *do* have formal veto power is influenced by the respective majority requirements stipulated in the constitution, namely simple majority, qualified majority, or unanimity (Tsebelis, 2000).

25 Tsebelis (1995: 311) distinguishes between cohesion and party discipline. The former

denotes positional differences within a party prior to their discussion, whereas the latter relates to the party's ability to subsequently control the votes of its MPs.

26 Treating partisan VPs as relevant in the dealings between upper and lower chambers in federal countries assumes that political parties are hierarchically organized from the national level downward. While this is certainly the case in Germany (and any other continental European country, for that matter), it does not hold in the Canadian case. The organization of parties, with the exception of the social democratic NDP, is clearly split between national and provincial levels, and parties do not exist on the municipal level at all.

27 These are understood as falling within the realm of Garrett and Lange's 'formal' public institutions, that is, they refer to governmental actors. In other words, corporatist top organizations do *not* qualify as informal components of Germany's Basic Law, as they of course are the incarnation of 'socioeconomic' institutions.

28 Duchacek conducts a second empirical test in which he then compares the term 'federal' to the actual working of those constitutions. I will, however, limit myself to his first test here.

29 He does not claim that the United States is the federal role model or the only 'true' federation; using the American system as the backdrop serves merely analytical purposes, as he considered the majority of his readers most familiar with it. Yet, as Duchacek emphasizes, the US constitution actually does not mention the term 'federalism' at all (1970: 207).

30 The other overlaps that blur the distinction between federal and provincial powers are: 1) the federal prerogative in defense; 2) emergency provisions; 3) concurrent powers; 4) elastic or coefficient clauses; and 5) the lack of precision in federal constitutions (see Duchacek, 1970: 258–73).

31 The rationale for constitutionally guaranteeing the powers of constituent units in federal states can be twofold: first, they often are societal, that is, rooted in language, culture and ethnicity. The second plausible cause is the organization of the welfare state through administrative and economic efficiency (Bakvis and Chandler, 1987b: 311). For a critical assessment of the former, see Riker (1964) and Cairns (1995). On federalism as the appropriate or deficient form of government for the latter, see Norrie (1995). Both aspects, of course, are not mutually exclusive, and many federations indeed display them in tandem. For the purposes of this book, only conditions pertaining to 'state-induced' federalism, that is, to the organization of the welfare state, are of relevance.

32 The Canadian provinces were briefed regularly by the representatives of the federal government during the negotiations of the NAFTA side agreements. In Germany, by contrast, even a formalized and substantive input by the Länder into the Maastricht negotiations through the Bundesrat had been established in the context of the preceding Single European Act in 1986 (cf. Müller-Brandeck-Bocquet, 1992). Yet, in both cases the constituent governments exerted their definitive influence at the domestic ratification (Germany) and implementation (Canada) stages, respectively.

33 Note that while the null hypothesis covers the entire analytical framework, the fiscal federalist hypotheses 'end' at the policy change, that is, they do *not* capture the feedback loop (Stage IV).

Chapter 4

Ratification Through Constitutional Change: Germany, the Single European Act and the Maastricht Treaty

> With this in mind, it would not, perhaps, be an exaggeration to suggest that prior to unification a largely unitary and centralized state form had been established behind the federal façade of the Federal Republic.
> Hartmut Klatt (1999: 56), 'Centralizing trends in West German federalism, 1949–89', in Charlie Jeffery (ed.), *Recasting German Federalism: The Legacies of Unification*, London: Pinter, pp. 40–57.

Along with Austria, whose economic relevance is limited, Germany is considered the most centralized federation among the OECD countries. This is not the case because Germany's constituent units, the Länder, did have limited competencies (as is the case with the Australian states). Instead, the unique feature is that the powers between Federation (*Bund*)[1] and Länder are divided along *functional* and *horizontal* lines. While the Bund is responsible for most legislation, the Länder are charged with the administration of federal laws. In return, the Länder take part in the enactment of all federal legislation through the second chamber, the Bundesrat, which represents the governments of the now 16 component units according to population size. Since the founding of the Federal Republic in 1949, the percentage of federal legislation that requires Bundesrat approval has risen from 40 to about 60 per cent.

This centralization was not originally intended in what used to be West Germany but rather developed over time, particularly in the late 1960s to mid-1970s. It was compounded not only in the wake of reunification in 1990 but particularly through the domestic legal changes following the two European treaties under investigation here. In that context, the Länder succeeded in further strengthening their *collective* influence via the Bundesrat in EU matters even in areas that previously fell under their *individual* jurisdiction domestically.

The first section of this chapter explains the reasons for the development toward centralization in West German federalism. It explores the historical context in which the constitution, labeled the 'Basic Law' (BL), was drafted in 1948/49, delineates the formal separation of powers between Federation and Länder, the bicameral arrangement and the resulting intergovernmental relations in their centralizing development over time. Section 2 outlines how and where the Single European Act (SEA) of 1986, which led to the completion of the Single European Market (SEM) by the end of 1992, impeded the powers of the German substates. Against this backdrop, the reaction of the Länder to the proposed treaty (Stage III of the Analytical Framework, see Figure 3.2), as well as their role in the domestic ratification of the SEA (Stage IV in Figure 3.2) are examined, before probing the implications for both the study's null hypothesis and the fiscal federalist hypotheses advanced in Chapter 2.

Finally, the topic of the third section is the Treaty on European Union (TEU), commonly referred to as the Maastricht Treaty, signed in 1991 and having come into effect on 1 January 1993. As the TEU clearly went beyond the Single European Act in its integrative scope, it prompted Länder involvement at an earlier stage and with noted impact on both the final treaty text as well as the domestic ratification process, resulting in constitutional changes to the Basic Law. Thus, for reasons of analytical consistency and to flesh out the marked differences between the two treaties, section 3 mimics the second one in structure.

German Federalism: Centralization in the Making

Historical Context

Although the geographical area now known as Germany has always been marked by an ethnically homogenous population as well as common cultural and linguistic traditions, for a long time it consisted of a patchwork varying from very extensive territorial units such as Prussia to city-states like Hamburg. It was not until 1871 that political unification through the establishment of the German Reich following the Franco-Prussian war was first achieved. The policy pursued by its mastermind, Bismarck, was to bring together the German states into a federation under the leadership of the Prussian monarchy.[2] In this federation of states (25 in all) the decisive role of Prussia was recognized through its dominant position in the institution which was formally sovereign, the Bundesrat, a chamber representing the governments of the member states.[3] Yet, despite Prussia's dominance, it also allowed the other states to retain considerable internal autonomy in the administration of domestic policies and services (Johnson, 1999: 26–7). This is the tradition in which the postwar (West) German constitution was drafted in 1948/49.[4]

The West Germans were asked, in line with the decisions of the London Conference in mid-1948, to prepare a constitution for the three Western zones. For its drafting, the occupying powers had provided instructions of only the most general nature. The key document did little more than require that the constitution to be drafted should protect individual rights, be based on democratic principles and provide for a federal structure of government.[5] The body, which was to prepare the constitution, was not to be a popularly elected constituent assembly. Instead, the Western allies preferred to build on the already existing Länder.[6] The Minister-Presidents of the Länder were charged with summoning such a body, which came to comprise 65 representatives of the *Landtage* (Länder parliaments) and was named 'Parliamentary Council'. After a certain amount of wrangling its final draft of March 1949 was accepted by the three Western powers, approved by all provincial parliaments except the Bavarian, and then promulgated as a 'provisional constitution', the so-called Basic Law (BL), on 23 May 1949.[7] Through it, the new Federal Republic of Germany was founded the following day.

The Länder were crucial for the particular form (West) German postwar federalism took and for its future development for two reasons. First, because the Basic Law was written *after* the Länder had already been established as effective political and administrative units, they could therefore influence the constitution of the Federal Republic in their favor. This meant a re-establishment, in the tradition of 1871, of the Bundesrat (rather than creating a Senate model) as a representation of the Länder executives according to population size with a significant legislative role, while leaving administration largely to the individual substates.

Second, the Länder as recreated after 1945 represented amalgamations of various regional particularisms, except in the cases of Hamburg, Bremen and Bavaria. Since the Western Allies wanted strong Länder in order to make impossible a strong centralized German state, they had offered the Länder Minister-Presidents the chance to restructure already prior to the deliberations on the founding of the Federal Republic. Yet, the Minister-Presidents had proved unable to convince their colleagues from the small and economically weak territories to agree to self-abolition.[8]

As a result, relations between the federal and Länder governments were marked by opposing interests among the Länder who were affected very unequally by wartime destruction and the number of refugees from what now had become parts of Poland and the Soviet Union.[9] While the specific postwar problems have naturally subsided, these initial differences in economic capabilities have influenced the development of German federalism until today. How the distinct similarities between the federal structure that was reestablished in 1949 with that of 1871, particularly in respect to the functional division of powers between the Federation and the Länder and role of the Bundesrat, underwent further centralization over the years is what we now turn to.

Formal Separation of Powers To understand the nature of German federalism compared to other federations, namely its *functional*, as opposed to vertical, separation of competencies between the two levels of government, one must distinguish between the administrative, legislative and fiscal powers as regulated in the Basic Law. The fourth aspect, that of treaty making, will be discussed later in the context of the SEA where it first became of crucial importance.

The Attribution of Administrative Functions The Länder have always been the main administrators not just of their own laws, but also of most federal and directly applicable European legislation. This is all the more important since the bulk of legislation is nowadays enacted at the federal or European level. Regarding the administrative role of the Länder, Articles 84 and 85 BL differentiate between administrative functions to be performed by the Länder 'as matters of their own concern', and other matters in which 'the Länder execute federal statutes as agents of the Federation'. The former are under general administrative rules requiring the Bundesrat's consent and subject to federal supervision relating to legal standards only, whereas the latter subject them 'to the instructions of the appropriate highest federal authorities' and to federal supervision dealing also with the 'appropriateness of execution' (Leonardy, 1999a: 10–11).[10]

The Distribution of Legislative Powers The bulk of legislation is today enacted at the federal level. This might seem paradoxical in the face of Art. 30 BL, which states that in general terms, 'except as otherwise provided or permitted by this Basic Law, the exercise of government powers and the discharge of governmental functions shall be incumbent on the Länder'. As has been shown above, this is still true in the administrative area. The paradox between reality and legal situation in the field of legislation is further sharpened through Art. 70 BL, which rules that 'the Länder shall have the right to legislate in so far as this Basic Law does not confer legislative power to the Federation' and thus defines the Länder as the location of residual legislative power. However, in the practical process of filling the statute books, this constitutional stipulation has been widely eroded in the legislative sphere. It has been caused by the impact of both the broadening of the criteria and the expansion of the catalogues of exclusive, concurrent and framework legislative powers of the federation in Articles 70 to 75 BL. This has had the effect of leaving a fairly small, though by no means unimportant, amount of legislative powers for the Länder, specifically in the areas of their own constitutions and of local government, policing, and cultural affairs including media legislation (Leonardy, 1999a: 12–13).

Among the categories of legislative powers of the federation, those of its concurrent and framework powers have been extended by numerous amendments to the Basic Law from 1949 onward.[11] The fields listed as concurrent and framework powers have been widened over the years, largely prompted by the so-called 'clause of need' (Art. 72/2 BL) that justifies federal concurrent and framework legislation in order to create a 'unity of living conditions throughout the country'.[12]

The 'Financial Constitution' The basic rule of the German 'financial constitution' (*Finanzverfassung*) is that the Federation and the Länder 'shall separately finance expenditure resulting from the discharge of their respective responsibilities in so far as this Basic Law does not provide otherwise' (Art. 104a BL). Yet, by 1955/56 the originally separated taxation powers of Bund and Länder were modified through the introduction of a system of joint income and corporation taxation, and both vertical (federal grants to the Länder) and horizontal (transfers among the Länder) financial equalization measures were expanded. In addition, sales (value-added) taxes were added to the catalogue of joint taxation provisions.[13] Finally, and most important, for some areas of policy, Bund-Länder cooperation was constitutionally secured in amendments to the Basic Law in 1969/70 (Articles 91 a–b and 104a BL), which introduced the so-called 'Joint Tasks' (*Gemeinschaftsaufgaben*). These are areas in which the federal and Länder governments engaged in shared planning, decision-making and financing, oriented toward the fulfillment of certain tasks for which the Länder originally had exclusive responsibility under the Basic Law. These projects and measures were concerned with economic and structural issues of national importance requiring heavy infrastructural investments which would, without the involvement of the Federation, place too great a financial burden on the Länder and municipalities.[14]

The important point here is that the Länder deliberately abandoned the autonomous competencies that the Basic Law had offered them. In particular, since they enjoyed concurrent legislative power for the majority of constitutional responsibilities, they would have been able to prevent the Federation from utilizing these competencies through their veto in the Bundesrat.[15] Yet, such blockades hardly ever occurred. Instead, the Länder governments agreed to a number of constitutional changes that extended federal powers and further limited the Länder in taking independent decisions. How can this be explained? From the perspective of the problem-ridden, economically weak and small Länder it made perfect sense to let the central state take on the expensive public tasks. However, all this could not have been in the interest of the big and financially powerful Länder; their aim was to redistribute tax revenues from the federal level to the Länder in order to enable the latter to fulfill expensive public services on their own.[16]

Given the unaltered distinction between have- and have-not Länder, combined with the constitutional mandate to create 'equal living conditions' across the country (Art. 72 BL), two interrelated 'laws' became evident. First, it depended on the small and poor Länder, and which tasks could be fulfilled by the substates independently and which ones had to be fully or partially taken on by the Federation. In other words, Bremen and Saarland determined the political room of maneuver for North Rhine-Westphalia and Bavaria. Second, the big and efficient Länder would agree to the extension of federal powers only on the condition that the Länder were at least guaranteed a right to a say in the execution of those competencies (Scharpf, 1994: 51). This had clear implications for the increasing power of the Bundesrat to which we now turn.

Bicameral Arrangement While the attribution of administrative, legislative and fiscal functions may sound to be a more or less technical matter, its significance within the German system derives from the implications that flow from it for the Bundesrat in the passing of federal legislation. It denotes the *horizontal* aspect of the German federal order and it consists of those cabinet members of the 16 Länder (11 before reunification) delegated to it by the respective Länder governments (Art. 51/1 BL). As in its predecessor of 1871, and in contrast to the Senate model, the Länder are not represented equally in terms of voting strength. Instead, the number of votes a Land has depends on its population size (Art. 51/2 BL), although this rule is tilted in favor of the smaller Länder.[17]

The main distinction to be made in the Bundesrat's role in federal legislation is that between laws that require its consent (*Zustimmungsgesetze* or 'consent bills') and those which do not. The latter nonetheless give the Bundesrat a suspensive veto of three weeks (*Einspruchsgesetze* or 'objection bills'). All bills that contain any financial implications for the Länder in implementing this legislation are consent bills, and all others are objection bills. As a result of the centralization and the 'Joint Tasks', the percentage of laws requiring Bundesrat approval has risen from about 40 per cent in the early 1950s to more than 60 per cent today (Goetz, 1995: 95).[18] In addition to the simple majorities needed for alterations of domestic laws, the Bundesrat must approve constitutional changes with a two-thirds majority. Should conflict arise between Bundestag and Bundesrat, the latter must demand that the so-called Mediation Committee (*Vermittlungsausschuß*) be convened in the case of objection bills. This constitutional organ (Art. 77/2 BL) consists of 16 representatives from the Bundesrat (one for each of the Länder) and the same number of members from the Bundestag.[19] By contrast, in the case of consent bills the Bundesrat can either convene the Mediation Committee or refuse its consent outright (Leonardy, 1999a: 14).

Reunification of the Federal Republic with the German Democratic Republic (GDR) in 1990 contributed further to the centralizing tendencies in German federalism.[20] The brevity in which the process was pushed through and the quick identification of East Germans with pre-1952 territorial structures effectively required the last independent GDR government to reinstate the five post-war Länder namely, Mecklenburg-Western Pomerania, Brandenburg, Saxony-Anhalt, Saxony and Thuringia. The attempt by the federal interior minister to completely overhaul the generally considered unpractical can-rule of territorial restructuring (Art. 29 BL; see n8) in the context of the reunification process met fierce resistance from the small West German Länder. Thus, it ultimately failed and the Federal Republic grew from 11 to 16 component units.

The five new Länder in the eastern part of the country with their average populations of three million belong to the small substates, and in the foreseeable future their economic power and tax revenues will remain far below the federal average. This had two interrelated consequences for the Bundesrat. One the one hand, the small Länder, that is, the economically and fiscally weak western substates, together with the new ones in the east, now clearly predominate the larger ones.[21] One the other hand, the four 'big' western Länder (Baden-Württemberg, Bavaria, Lower Saxony and North Rhine-Westphalia) achieved a reapportionment of votes in the Bundesrat to retain a blocking minority (one-third of the total Bundesrat votes) in respect of constitutional legislation.

In West German federalism the interests of the central government and the small and financially weak Länder had already converged, resulting in the financial reform of 1969 with its increase in federal competencies. Yet, since the execution depended on the consent of all or almost all Länder, this forced the federal government to treat all component units equally. Scharpf (1994: 55) charges that the accession of five economically and fiscally weak East German Länder further accelerates this development and bring the country 'a big step closer to a *de facto* centralized state that is merely made more expensive and complicated through the existence of the Länder' (my translation).[22]

Resulting Intergovernmental Relations

While the Bundesrat embodies intergovernmentalism at the regional level, the practical operation of any federal system as a whole also requires that intergovernmental relations are conducted between all levels of government. First, what is termed the 'whole state' (*Gesamtstaat*) comprises institutions in which both the Federation and the Länder are represented on terms of equal status. This allows no room for majority decision-making but necessitates accommodation and compromise. The 'top' institution is the Conference of the Heads of Governments of the Federation and the Länder. These are conferences held between the Federal Chancellor and the Minister-Presidents of the Länder in a more or less regular sequence of roughly every four months.

Second, the level of the 'Federal state' (*Bundesstaat*) consists of the constitutionally organized structure of interrelationships between the Federation and the Länder institutions, whose decisions are subject to majority voting rules. The subject matter of all such decisions must be located within the field of federal competence, or must be subject to federal procedures (as in the case of the 'Joint Tasks'). The Bundesrat is, of course, at the center of the structure; its role is also indicative of Germany's 'unitary' and 'cooperative' federalism in its institutionalized need for broad consensus. Neither can federal or Länder governments impose policies on each other, nor can the Länder gain leverage in the Federation without agreement among themselves (Goetz, 1995: 95).

Finally, there is the level of horizontal coordination between the Länder themselves, which in a strict sense is not part of the relations between the Federation and the Länder, but without which neither the decisions of the 'Federal state' nor those of the 'whole state' could be properly prepared. This area is commonly known as the 'Third Level' where decisions, whether dealing with federal or Länder matters, must be taken unanimously. The highest-ranking institution is the Conference of the Minister-Presidents, which meets formally once a year, but convenes in practice almost monthly and always before the Conference with the Federal Chancellor at the 'whole state'.[23]

Goetz (1995: 93) condensed five characteristics of German intergovernmental relations. First, rather than being clearly separated between levels of government, the vast majority of powers are *shared* between Federation and component units. Second, this has led to a high degree of both vertical and horizontal *joint* policy-making. Third, Germany is marked by extensive legal centralization through the dominance of national laws. Fourth, as a 'counterweight', the implementation of federal legislation is primarily in the hands of the Länder, although implementation *itself* is subject to considerable uniformity (Müller-Brandeck-Bocquet, 1992: 167–8). Fifth, the coordination between levels of government exclusively involves their political and administrative executives.[24]

Intergovernmental relations in Germany were set to be heavily affected by increased European economic integration as treaties began to encroach upon Länder competencies. It is this aspect that we now turn to for the remainder of this chapter.

The Single European Act: First Impediments on Länder Powers

Purpose and Contents of the Treaty

As briefly indicated in Chapter 3, 'Eurosclerosis' was the term coined in the late 1970s to describe two related phenomena: first, the political stagnation of further economic integration in the European Community (EC),[25] and second, the poor competitiveness of most European economies *vis-à-vis* those of the United States and Japan. The SEA was adopted on 26 February 1986 to alleviate both problems;[26] its core is the single market (SEM) program, which is based on the assumption that non-tariff barriers to trade between member states were the major cause of the economic component of Eurosclerosis.[27] The single market is defined in the SEA as 'an area without internal frontiers in which the free movement of goods, persons, services and capital is ensured'. Clarifying these so-called four freedoms, the SEM encompasses eight different aspects.

First, the elimination of *technical barriers* was to be achieved through two components: mutual recognition of national standards; and approximation through the stipulation of Union-wide 'essential requirements' such as minimum safety and health standards. The intended effect of these principles was to prevent national standards from being used as impediments to cross-border trade. Second, the reduction of *fiscal barriers* was deemed necessary, as differences in indirect taxes, in particular the valued added tax and excise duties, were also regarded as major obstacles to cross-border trade. Given the wide disparities in tax systems within the Community, the aim was to approximate rather than to fully harmonize indirect taxes.

Third, the removal of *physical barriers* concerns especially the abolition of customs forms and formalities. While over 150 previous documents in use for the transport of goods across EC internal borders were replaced by a single one by January 1988, even this was abrogated by January 1993. The liberalization of transport services has been a key element in the program, particularly regarding to the elimination of quota restrictions on road shipments.

Fourth, nationals of any member state have the right to seek and obtain *employment* anywhere in the Community. They also mostly enjoy the same treatment as nationals of the respective host states in matters of payment, working conditions, and trade union rights. Fifth, professionals in many *occupations* now have the right to have their qualifications recognized in other member states.

Sixth, *financial services* have been opened, that is, cross-border restrictions on the operation of businesses in the services sector, such as banking and insurance, were largely eliminated. Seventh, arrangements for the free *movement of capital* now apply throughout the EC. Eighth, various directives have been introduced to open *public procurement* markets. According to the European Commission public purchasing has reached up to 15 per cent of Gross Domestic Product (GDP), while in the mid-1980s only 2 per cent of all government contracts went to suppliers from other EC countries.[28]

To accomplish the goals of the single market, the SEA contains two sets of additional novelties: first, the *institutional* innovation was the adoption of qualified majority voting (QMV) in the European Council for all measures related to the establishment of the single market.[29] According to the European Commission, 279 EC directives were required to accomplish the SEM by the end of 1992, which had to be approved by the Council to become law in the member states.[30] Second, the market-enhancing scheme of the single market was *substantially* complemented in the SEA in three ways: first, in cooperation between European industry and the Commission, an 'imitation of Japanese technology corporatism' (Parker, 2000) was established. Second, the 'building up a supranational cohesion regime through the revised and extended regional policy' is considered a side payment to garner enough support for the single market program among member states (Ziltener, 2000a). Third, although building the weakest part of the SEA, EC competencies in social regulations have been expanded and strengthened. The treaty provides an explicit legal basis for environmental protection and the inclusion of this component in all other Community policies (Art. 130r EC Treaty). In addition, it also introduced QMV for issues of occupational health and safety, as well as for the working environment. EC directives in these fields do not need to be explicitly justified with the completion of the internal market (Majone, 1993: 164; Springer, 1992; Ziltener, 2000b).[31]

Encroachment on Länder Competencies

The provisions for the completion for the internal market have an expansive logic, that is, economic regulations cannot be restricted in their relevance and thereby clearly affect non-economic areas. For instance, to take two quarrels between the Community and the Länder, television is not only a means of political communication and of cultural identity formation but also a service for which market access can be regulated at the European level. Also, the right to vote in municipal elections is not only a matter of Länder competencies in drawing up 'municipal constitutions' but it also has an impact on the free movement of labor in the common market. In a similar vein, the recognition of education, vocational training, waste management and worker codetermination at the plant level are of such obvious relevance for the openness of the common market that European regulations in these areas cannot be resisted with legally convincing arguments (Scharpf, 1994: 123).

Apart from the completion of the common market, the SEA includes extensions of earlier Community authority, especially in the field of social policy (e.g. working conditions and minimum standards), and the introduction of new EC responsibilities in the areas of research and technology as well as the environment. With the harmonizing of many regulations as well as tax systems, important changes also occurred in the fields of health and consumer protection. Through the new responsibilities of the Community, core competencies of the Länder also became part of European harmonization attempts; this particularly relates to education and research as well as culture. Yet, probably the most crucial aspect of EC intrusion in Länder competencies concerns regional economic policy (*Regionalförderung*).[32] Thus, the extension of European tasks and functions through the SEA did not so much consist of the schematic transfer of competencies from member states to Brussels. Rather it was the acquisition by the EC of co-responsibility and of possibilities of co-determination with the member states in ever more policy areas (Hrbek, 1999: 218).

There are three threats that arose for the German Länder in particular. The first challenge emanated from the fact that a number of policy areas are ones reserved for the Länder in the internal allocation of competencies in Germany. This applies for example to the fields of culture and the media, education and training, health, the environment, research and technology, and, in particular, regional structural policy. In this field the Länder especially have to observe the EC subsidy control regime (Articles 92 to 94 of the EC Treaty). The activity of the Community in these fields and the incorporation of the Länder into this wider supranational framework have the effect of considerably limiting the autonomy of the Länder to structure politics and policy within their territories.

The second challenge has arisen from the modalities of decision-making in EC affairs. The most important body in this respect has always been – and still is – the Council of Ministers, in which Germany is represented by the federal government. The latter has therefore participated in decisions in fields that not only impinged on Länder concerns but also, in part, their exclusive powers. While the federal government possesses no internal decision-making competence in such fields, it has the possibility and duty externally to participate in such processes under the terms of Community law.

Here, the Länder are affected in a further respect. Within the German federal system they have extensive powers of implementation and their rights of participation in federal legislation give them the possibility of codetermining implementation rules. Although they are also responsible for the implementation of European law, they have lacked the possibility of participating in legislation and come under a much stronger degree of control by the federal government, which is responsible to the Community institutions for ensuring proper implementation of European legislation (Hrbek, 1999: 218–19). Hence, the compensation of a loss of competencies by the Länder through extended co-decision rights in the Bundesrat that had been used domestically does not work anymore when the powers in question are transferred further from the national level to Brussels (Scharpf, 1994: 55).

Stage III: Länder Reaction and Effect on Treaty

The regulation of treaty-making powers in the Basic Law explains how Länder powers could be transferred to the supranational level in the first place; three articles are key in determining the roles of federal and component governments in this respect. According to Art. 32/1 BL, the federal government is the sole representative of Germany abroad and conducts relations with foreign countries. In addition, Art. 24/1 BL allows the federal government to transfer powers to supranational institutions, even if these powers domestically fall under Länder jurisdiction. This is possible without their consent, for most changes could be introduced as simple federal laws over which the Bundesrat only has a suspensive veto (Jeffery, 1996: 254–5).[33] The Federation merely has to observe Art. 79/3 BL (the so-called eternity clause), which renders inadmissible any constitutional changes that eliminate the federal order.[34] The federal government as the representative in the Council of Ministers then participates in EU decision-making which can further curtail Länder powers; nonetheless, the Länder are obliged to implement European law in the Federal Republic.[35] Hence, through European integration the federal balance has tilted in favor of the Federation (Burgess and Gress, 1993: 169–70).[36]

On this basis, it is not surprising that for the Länder Art. 24/1 BL was the 'open flank' of German federalism. First, given the intrusion of decisions taken in Brussels on national policy making, they charged that relations with the Community no longer constitute traditional external affairs (in the sense of Art. 32/1 BL), over which the Federation has the undisputed prerogative. Second, and closely related, if the federal government increasingly relinquishes competencies to the EC that domestically fall under Länder jurisdiction, then this undermines the guarantee of the federal order under Art. 79/3 BL. Therefore, with the tensions between Articles 24/1, 32/1 and 79/3 of the Basic Law, the Länder held that EC policies must be treated as domestic policy; thus, they would fall under Art. 50 BL, which stipulates that through the Bundesrat the Länder participate in federal decision-making.

The Länder have pursued two avenues, apart from defensive protest about the 'flood of regulations' emanating from the European Commission, to halt the erosion of their competencies: first, they attempted to strengthen their possibilities of participation *vis-à-vis* the federal government. Second, since the mid-1980s the Länder have taken a direct route to the EC institutions by opening their own liaison offices in Brussels.

Regarding Länder participation in the internal development of the federal government's position in the Council of Ministers, there were two predecessors to changes in the context of the SEA. First, already with the ratification of the Rome Treaties in 1957, the federal government was obliged to constantly inform the Länder about developments at the European level. On this basis, the Bundesrat had the opportunity to present opinions on proposed EC legislation. In the absence of any appropriate legal foundation, it was not, however, guaranteed that the federal government would take such opinions into account in discussions in Community bodies.

Second, in an exchange of letters between the Federal Chancellor and the President of the Conference of Minister-Presidents in 1979, the federal government committed itself to delivering more comprehensive information to the Länder at an earlier stage. It also declared itself prepared to follow Länder views strictly if their competencies were affected, and if no 'foreign or integration policy' concerns stood in the way (Hrbek, 1999: 220–21).

In parallel, the Länder have engaged in independent EC activities since the mid-1980s to reflect the growing influence of Community decisions on subnational policies. Most relevant among these measures, they have opened information offices between 1985 and 1987 (see Hooghe, 1995; Marks *et al.*, 1996), with the eastern Länder later following their example. The offices were initially subject to federal government criticism that they represented 'auxiliary foreign policy' (*Nebenaußenpolitik*), but are now perceived and treated as normal.[37] The functions of the information offices are diverse. They secure and pass information, are involved in the economic promotion of their Land and assist firms and other bodies in the development of projects in which EC institutions play a role (Hrbek, 1999: 225–6).

Stage IV: Ratification of the SEA

In 1986, the Bundesrat used the opportunity to strengthen its participation in the course of the Law of Ratification of the SEA, whose constitutional necessity, it must be emphasized, was at best disputed. Nonetheless, the federal government voluntarily conceded to Bundesrat consent for the ratification of the treaty (Müller-Brandeck-Bocquet, 1992: 173; Scharpf, 1994: 93), which the Länder exploited to expand and above all legally entrench their internal rights of participation. The Law was passed on 19 December 1986 and, together with the supplementary Federal-Länder Agreement concluded in 1987, it exhibits the following provisions. Art. 2/1 SEA Law reinforces the duty of the federal government to inform the Bundesrat about all its projects that could be of interest to the Länder comprehensively and at the earliest possible time. According to Art. 2/2 the federal government allows the Bundesrat to voice its opinion on matters affecting important Länder interests within reasonable time. This meant that the Bundesrat attempt to *oblige* the federal government to seek its opinion in all matters of exclusive Länder competence had failed. The federal government had rejected the Bundesrat proposal as not conforming to the exclusive responsibility of the Federation for foreign affairs (Art. 32 BL).

The most important and controversial regulation of the Ratification Law concerns the binding of the federal government to Bundesrat opinions. Art. 2/3 requires the federal government to take Bundesrat comments into account and deviate from them, in cases falling under the exclusive legislative competence of the Länder, only for unavoidable reasons of foreign and integration policy. Should such an instance occur, the federal government must explain the reasons for the deviation (Art. 2/4 SEA Law). Finally, an additional long-standing point of contention between Federation and Länder was the increased participation of Länder representatives in the federal negotiating delegations in Brussels. Art. 2/5 SEA Law now obliges the federal government to call in Land representatives at the negotiation stage in the Council and Commission if exclusive Länder competencies are at stake, 'to the extent that this is possible for the Federal Government' (Nass, 1989: 179).[38] All the details on the above regulations were to be filled by a Federation-Länder Agreement that was concluded in December 1987 (Art. 2/6 SEA Law). According to this, the Bundesrat has to nominate the Länder representatives for the German EC delegations.

In this context, on 10 June 1988 the Bundesrat established a 'European Chamber' in which all Länder have one representative (unlike the plenary), and which has its own decision-making power (unlike all other Bundesrat committees). This was considered important because Community regulations already accounted for about one third of all Bundesrat matters at the time (Müller-Brandeck-Bocquet, 1992: 173–5). In addition, stronger Länder involvement in the federal government's EC negotiating position meant, first, that decisions often have to be made within a timeframe that does not allow waiting for the next plenary session. Second, meetings of the Europe Chamber are not public, so as not to compromise the development of a German negotiating position.

In other words, from now on the Bundesrat was clearly at the center of European activities by the Länder. This decision by the Länder to voluntarily opt for the Bundesrat procedure in EC affairs is a further extension of the horizontal separation of powers in German federalism. Although it therefore appears to have been an expected move by the Länder to opt for this solution, it is significant none the less since for the first time they deviated from the principle of Länder unanimity in areas that domestically fall under their jurisdiction. Additionally, it must be noted the rules for Bundesrat participation in Community affairs cannot with any confidence be considered a replacement of the domestic veto position enjoyed by the Bundesrat simply because the federal government itself can be overruled in the Council of Ministers (Scharpf, 1994: 55).

Implications for the Null Hypothesis and the Fiscal Federalist Hypotheses

The study's null hypothesis, positing that domestic institutional factors did *not* play a role in the establishment of the SEA, cannot be rejected with confidence. The Länder established liaison offices in Brussels, initially in opposition to the federal government. In addition, and more important, the federal government subjected the SEA to Bundesrat approval, although it was unclear whether this move was constitutionally imperative. Nevertheless, both Länder 'successes' were only controversial domestically; they did not have any impact on the SEA treaty as such. This, however, was the criterion for the mediating role of extant domestic institutions set out in Chapter 3. At the same time, a rejection of the null hypothesis in this instance would also not be consistent with the propositions by both Garrett and Lange and Fiscal Federalism. They lead us to expect that a rather centralized political system should be able to enact institutional adjustment with little or no opposition due to a lack of institutional veto players. The only possible veto player in this case, the Bundesrat, did not, despite the clear infringements on Länder competencies, contemplate opposing the treaty once granted the right to ratify the SEA. Instead, the Ratification Law, in the tradition of German federalism, was marked by its collective (that is, strengthening the Bundesrat rather than the Länder) and essentially consensual (with the federal government) style.

Turning to the fiscal federalist hypotheses, it becomes clear that the purpose of the single market was the creation of a regulatory framework to strengthen the efficiency of resource allocation by allowing Community-wide competition and the increased realization of economies of scale in the private sector. The twelve EC member states at the time had by far become each other's main trading partners with 60 per cent of their exports going to each other by 1989 (Keohane and Hoffmann, 1991: 1). Yet, the existing institutional framework was detrimental for EU producers as a whole *vis-à-vis* their American and Japanese competitors. The means for institutional adjustment was to deregulate the above sectors domestically mostly through the use of the concept of 'mutual recognition'; all member states had to allow goods and services produced under the standards of anyone member state to enter their national markets.[39] This is consistent with the third fiscal federalist hypothesis advanced in Chapter 2. It leads us to expect that the higher the degree of mutual interdependence between countries, the stronger is the impetus for these countries to enhance the allocative efficiency of both the private and public sector through the supranationalization of regulatory public goods.

Ratifying the Maastricht Treaty: Altering the Constitution

Purpose and Contents of the Treaty

The Treaty on European Union (TEU), signed in Maastricht on 7 February 1992 and having come into force on 1 November 1993, marks not only a terminological shift from 'Community' to 'Union'; substantively, it comprises seven Titles and rests on three so-called pillars: the first consists of the EC Treaty with its amendments; most of them are contained in the 238 articles of Title II, thus forming 'a treaty within the treaty'.[40] They cover new or extended EU responsibilities in economic and monetary policy, social policy, education, vocational training, culture, public health, consumer protection, industry, economic and social cohesion, the environment, research and technology. Second, a Common Foreign and Security Policy (CFSP) is envisioned with its various purposes defined in the Treaty (Title V).[41] Third, the realm of Justice and Home Affairs (JHA) covers intergovernmental cooperation on immigration, asylum, fraud, civil matters, as well as police cooperation to prevent and combat terrorism, drug trafficking and other forms of international crime (Title VI).[42] CFSP and JHA are intergovernmental pillars, excluding these policy areas included in normal EU decision-making.[43]

Two aspects are commonly regarded as the most important elements of the Maastricht Treaty: the provisions and protocols relating to the Economic and Monetary Union (EMU), and the considerable extensions regarding social and economic cohesion, better known as EU regional policy. The move toward a single European currency was seen as a logical consequence of the single market program adopted with the SEA. The free movement of goods, services, capital and labor proved to be clearly curtailed by the vagaries of exchange rate fluctuations. In addition, a common currency would effectively prevent states with such an extraordinary high degree of cross-border trade from using their currencies as instruments of economic policy, that is, for competitive devaluations in order to promote their respective export industries.[44]

Apart from the stabilization function of EMU, additional financial means to increase the redistribution of income between European regions have been introduced with the Maastricht Treaty. Until the creation of the European Regional Development Fund (ERDF) in 1975, following the entry of the UK and Ireland, regional policy within the Union was largely a prerogative of the member states. The accession of Spain and Portugal doubled the number of people that were living in regions that have a per capita income of less than 75 per cent of the Union average. Hence, a Union-wide regional policy is primarily an issue of reducing equity differences in living standards, as poorer regions tend to have a smaller endowment with immobile factors of production.[45]

The Union's *structural funds* are the main financial instruments for pursuing the aims of greater economic and social cohesion within the Union. ERDF assistance is provided both in the form of grants for specific projects, and as program assistance, which can cover a broader range of measures targeted at specific problems over several years. It has grown from 4.5 per cent of Union spending in 1975 to 13.1 per cent in 1995 and operates on the basis of the so-called additionality principle, meaning that allocations should be additional to funding provided by national governments. The funds have been reformed several times, seeking to ensure closer coordination of structural policies by setting common objectives. In December 1992, parallel to the official completion of the single market, the European Council in Edinburgh earmarked ECU141.5 billion for the regions between 1993 and 1999. Including funding for the 1995 entrants, the total has been increased to about ECU150 billion between 1994 and 1999.[46]

In addition, the *Cohesion Fund* was established at the Maastricht summit, due to strong pressure from the four poorest member states (Portugal, Spain, Greece and Ireland, with a combined population of 63 million). The TEU includes a protocol on economic and social cohesion and requires the Fund to provide financial support for transport and environmental infrastructure projects.[47] Hence, whereas the ERDF attempts to reduce regional disparities at large, the project-based Cohesion Fund seeks to reduce disparities between member states. In 1992, the above four countries received 50 per cent of the funds. Together with the Cohesion Fund, this portion increased to 54 per cent by 1999.

Encroachment on Länder Competencies

It is clear that both monetary policy and CFSP fall under federal jurisdiction, so Länder interests are not at all at stake. By contrast, the references of Title II of the TEU collectively constitute a significant extension of the Community's policy responsibilities beyond the SEA. 'Since Maastricht, there is scarcely a [Länder] policy area which is not, at least in part, dealt within the framework of the EU' (Hrbek, 1999: 218). Furthermore, aspects of JHA, in particular police service, fall squarely into Länder competencies.

Stage III: Länder Reaction and Effect on Treaty

The Länder have never left any doubt about their positive commitment to the European integration process and their support for its further development and institutional deepening. They have supplemented this general commitment with concrete views on how this union should be created and on what structural principles it should be based.

The starting point of a series of initiatives following the ratification of the SEA was the resolution of the Minister-Presidents' Conference in Munich in October 1987, where the goal of 'a Europe with federal structures' was formulated. Two years later the Minister-Presidents established a working group to recommend the position the Länder should adopt in the further development of the EC. The report, presented in May 1990, contained concrete proposals for revisions to the community treaties. They were then distilled into four points: the incorporation of the subsidiarity principle; models for the participation of the Länder and regions in the Council of Ministers; the creation of a 'regional organ' at the supranational level; and the introduction of an independent right of appeal for the Länder and regions to the European Court of Justice. These demands were confirmed in a resolution of the Minister-Presidents on 7 June 1990 and in a Bundesrat resolution of 24 August that year. In addition, the federal government was called upon in the Bundesrat resolution to involve the Länder in the work of the intergovernmental conference (which conceived what later became the Maastricht Treaty), including the preparatory discussions that would define the German negotiating position.[48] The four Länder demands were ultimately reflected in the TEU in the following way.

The Subsidiarity Principle The wording of the subsidiarity principle[49] in Art. 3b/2 EC Treaty only went as far as the relationship between the Community and the member states were concerned; it left the regional level out of consideration. The ambiguous legal concepts in the formulation – 'not sufficiently' and 'better' – raised doubt about whether the subsidiarity principle is usable in this formulation as a justiciable basis for any appeal or whether it can ultimately, if at all, develop any restraining political effect.

Direct Länder Participation in the Council of Ministers The Maastricht Treaty revised Art. 146 EC Treaty, which determines the composition of the Council of Ministers; it now allows for the possibility that a Länder delegate can represent the Federal Republic in this body.

The Creation of the Committee of the Regions (CoR) The demand of the Länder for a 'regional organ' was only imperfectly fulfilled with the creation of this new institution. The Committee is restricted to merely advisory functions. Its organizational infrastructure and its financial resources are extremely modest. But the main weakness is the wide heterogeneity in its composition. The 'regions' represented differ markedly in terms of legal status and political quality. CoR will therefore find it hard to develop an autonomous profile and grow into a role as a noteworthy player in the European decision-making process. Also, not all of the 24 German seats in

CoR were reserved for the Länder; three seats have been allocated to the three peak organizations of German local government.[50]

The Right of Appeal to the European Court of Justice (ECJ) Neither individual regions nor the CoR were awarded an independent right of appeal to the ECJ in the Maastricht Treaty. If the Länder wish to pursue an appeal, for example against decisions of the Commission, they have to rely on the cooperation of the federal government.[51]

Stage IV: Ratification of the Maastricht Treaty

Since the provisions of theTEU, unlike the SEA, indisputably amended the Basic Law, the Länder used the opportunity of its ratification to strengthen their position *vis-à-vis* the EU decision-making process of the federal government. The Basic Law was altered and amended in several places to ensure that federal constitutional law would be fully compatible with the stipulations of the Maastricht Treaty; these changes came into force on 21 December 1992. In terms of domestic intergovernmental relations, two changes are of particular importance; they relate to Articles 50 and 23 BL. First, Art. 50 BL previously read: 'The Länder shall participate through the Bundesrat in the legislative process and administration of the Federation'. It has now been added: 'and in matters concerning the European Union'. Thus, for the first time the Basic Law explicitly acknowledges the right of the Länder to participate in the legislation and administration of the EU; obtaining such a clear constitutional foundation was a long-held Länder claim.

Second, a new Art. 23 BL has been inserted, which is commonly referred to as the 'Article on European Union'; it specifies and extends the participatory rights of the Länder. There are three novelties that are of special importance: Art. 23/1 BL determines that '[t]he establishment of the European Union as well as amendments to its statutory foundations and comparable regulations which amend or supplement the contents of this Basic Law or make such amendments or supplements possible shall be subject to the provisions of paragraphs (2) and (3) of Article 79'. These procedural conditions for the further development of the EU were an important innovation, for Art. 79/2 mandates approval by a two-thirds majority in the Bundesrat (and the Bundestag); hitherto the basis for the transfer of competencies had been Art. 24/1 BL ('The Federation may by legislation transfer sovereign powers to intergovernmental institutions').[52]

Building on the provisions of the SEA Ratification Law, Art. 23/5 BL stipulates that whenever Länder interests are affected but the Federation has exclusive legislative jurisdiction, the Bundesrat opinion has to be 'taken into account'. In contrast, where Länder legislative powers and administrative procedures are at stake, the Bundesrat opinion 'shall in this respect prevail in the decision-making process of the Federation'. Yet, if such a position has negative financial implications for the Federation, the federal government's consent is required. Finally, Art. 23/6 BL regulates that in matters of exclusive legislative Länder jurisdiction, the exercise of the rights of the Federal Republic of Germany as a member state of the European Union shall be transferred by the Federation to a representative of the Länder designated by the Bundesrat'. The delegate in question will work in close cooperation with the federal government, ensuring that representation of the Federation *as a whole* is maintained.

The Bund-Länder Cooperation Law of 12 March 1993, in conjunction with the Agreement between the Federal and Länder Governments of 29 October 1993, regulated the details of Art. 23 BL. § 5/2 of the Cooperation Law specifies Art. 23/5 BL such that wherever Länder legislative powers and administrative procedures are at stake, the federal government shall take the Bundesrat opinion 'decisively' into account. In case of disagreement between federal government and Bundesrat, the two sides still seek to reach a compromise. If that fails, and the Bundesrat confirms its view by a two-thirds majority vote, then the federal government is *obliged* to hold to the Bundesrat view.[53] § 5/3 Cooperation Law relates to measures taken by the Council of Ministers based on Art. 235 EC Treaty, often known as the *Kompetenz-Kompetenz*, the 'competence to define competencies' (see also n.37). It allows the EU to take action even when it is not explicitly empowered by the EC Treaty to do so, if the member state governments are unanimously of the view in the Council that the respective measure should be taken to realize the aims of the Common Market. § 5/3 Cooperation Law now mandates that in such cases federal government approval now has to be backed by the consent of the Bundesrat.[54]

Under § 6/1 Cooperation Law, the federal government allows Länder representatives nominated by the Bundesrat on a case-by-case basis to form part of the German delegation in the Council and the Commission.[55] Furthermore, § 6/2 Cooperation Law clarifies if the matter concerned 'centrally affects exclusive legislative competencies of the Länder', the lead role in the negotiations for the German delegation is transferred to Länder representative; yet, the Bundesrat must nominate a Länder emissary of cabinet rank in this instance.

It follows, again, that the application of these rules requires cooperation and compromise. First, it is *not* the individual Länder but the collective institution of the Bundesrat that collaborates with the federal government, thus requiring a consensual Länder position. The clear economic differences among the Länder have not prevented them from pursuing a common line (Goetz, 1995: 110). Second, the same holds for the relationship between federal government and Bundesrat with the new Art. 23 BL. Given this, EU integration has left the characteristics of German intergovernmental relations intact. This is not to say, however, that it has not initiated considerable adaptability pressures, as can be seen in the strategy pursued by the Länder in the context of the Maastricht Treaty.

Implications for the Null Hypothesis and the Fiscal Federalist Hypotheses

Contrary to the assessment following the SEA, the null hypothesis can be clearly rejected here. The Länder have significantly influenced the federal government's negotiating position at Maastricht, having adopted the Länder demands of a regional chamber, the principle of subsidiarity and representation of the Federal Republic in the Council through a Länder representative in case of exclusive substate competencies being at stake.[56] Consent of the Bundesrat to ratify the Maastricht Treaty was achieved through constitutional changes to the Basic Law. It is on this basis that Hrbek (1999: 229) asserts that, contrary to many scholarly depictions, the Länder have *not* been the losers in the process of EU integration.

In terms of Fiscal Federalism, Hypothesis 1 postulates that the higher the degree of financial capital mobility (monetary policy) and mutual economic interdependence (fiscal policy) between countries, the more likely is the stabilization function to be shifted upwards. As far as monetary policy is concerned, one of the eight policies ratified with the SEA was to enhance capital mobility beyond the 'normal' degree associated with globalization by further deregulating the financial sector. Frieden (1997) confirms this hypothesis by observing that the domestic pressure generated by the SEM for monetary integration is a function of the level of economic integration among EU member states in general, and within the DM-zone in particular.[57] Put differently, the practical interconnectedness of the three public sector functions (Oates, 1972: xv) effectively predetermined the installation of a common currency after deregulation of capital mobility with the SEA.[58] In contrast, despite a certain degree of tax harmonization established with the SEA, fiscal policy has *not* been supranationalized. As was pointed out above, the mutual economic interdependence between member states of the Euro zone is undoubtedly 'high' compared to the relationship with non-EU countries. Yet it still is lower than financial capital mobility among the member states on the one hand, and the economic ties *within* EU countries on the other. Hence, the first hypothesis finds its limitations in this case.

Hypothesis 2 associates a supranationalization of the distribution function with enhanced mobility of residents across national borders. While the SEA has lifted restrictions on occupation and moved toward mutual recognition of education degrees, very few EU inhabitants make use of the increased *potential* for mobility across among the member states, not least due to the language barriers. Thus, it is consistent with the second hypothesis not to expect EU-wide income redistribution on the individual level for many years to come.

Yet, given the low individual mobility, *regional* income distribution is, apart from being politically more feasible, very useful. As Padoa-Schioppa (1995) has pointed out, the increase of structural and Cohesion funds with the SEA and especially the TEU can be attributed to the fact that while some EU regions were better off with the provisions of both SEA and TEU, several regions/member states were worse off. In other words, enhancing allocative efficiency through regulatory public goods and monetary policy had violated the criterion of Pareto-optimality. Of course, the *revenues* that the EU is able to acquire are crucial for any redistributive means. To date the EU itself, however, has no tax power; rather it receives what can be seen as intergovernmental grants from the member states (Boadway and Keen, 1997). Padoa-Schioppa (1995) stresses that the way in which member states contributions to the EU budget are differentiated qualifies as a redistributive mechanism in itself.

In summation, Germany as an extremely centralized federation with its *functional* division of powers has adapted to the considerable threats posed for Länder competencies in a rather smooth manner; it did not exhibit confrontations between the Bund and the Länder. To the contrary, the centralizing tendency through further powers for the federal institution of the Bundesrat at the expense of individual Länder responsibilities has continued unabated, enabling constitutional change to ratify the Maastricht Treaty. This broadly confirms the fiscal federalist as well as Garrett and Lange's expectations that a centralized political system, that is, one with few institutional veto players, should be in a good position to institutionally adapt to external changes. How Canada as the incarnation of a decentralized federation fares in this respect is the question we turn to in the following chapter.

Notes

1 I capitalize the term 'federation' if it coincides with the German designation 'Bund', meaning national agencies as opposed to subnational (that is, Länder) ones. If it is used as an equivalent of a federal state in the generic sense, the noun 'federation' remains uncapitalized.

2 With three-fifths of the population, Prussia constituted a powerful state within the state. It was formally dissolved by the occupying powers in 1947, which is perhaps a unique example of the abolition of a state by formal decree.

3 The immediate participation of the subnational governments in the policy-making of the Reich also explains why the Bundesrat could not also be developed as a bulwark against continued centralization of responsibilities and competencies; there is no need to constrain government if you share in the power.

4 Given the increasing gulf between the western powers and the Soviet Union after the Second World War, it was only in the western zones of the former German state that an autonomous political reconstruction could take place. Anxious to reduce the burdens of occupation and to secure West German support for their resistance against the Soviet threat, the three Western powers were by 1948 ready to envisage the reestablishment of a German state within the area they administered.

5 They left the interpretation of these requirements to the constitution-making body, though reserving for themselves full rights of approval of whatever draft constitution might ultimately be submitted. It was thus a thoroughly German constitutional document.

6 The three Western powers discovered even before the end of 1945 that they needed German administrative agents. In a remarkably short time, with the United States as pacemaker, all of them created within their zones provincial governments which were, in

most cases, quickly legitimized by holding elections and the drafting of Land constitutions. The Länder administrations were, therefore, the only effective instruments of government at the time the constitution was being drafted, and on this account alone their influence on the final settlement was substantial (Johnson, 1999: 31–2).

7 The provisional character was not due to any objections by the Western allies. Instead, the preamble of the Basic Law stated that only the whole German populace could establish a constitution at a future point in time. This was a political statement demanding all West German governments to work toward the goal of reunification. In this context, the Federal Republic never recognized the GDR, founded on 7 October 1949, as a foreign state. Hence, it did not have an embassy in East Berlin but only a 'permanent presentation'.

8 In the 'Document No. II' from 1 July 1948, the Allies called on the Minister-Presidents to propose alterations to the Länder boundaries and thereby avoid the creation of Länder that are either too big or too small in comparison to other Länder. Instead, as early as 10 July 1948 the Minister-Presidents recommended postponing territorial restructuring as a whole until a later date. The only exception combined the three south-western Länder in 1951 to form Baden-Württemberg, a prospect already provided specifically by Art. 118 BL. It has since become one of the economically most powerful Länder. In 1973, the Commission for Territorial Restructuring that had been set up by the Minister of the Interior proposed several options that would have reduced the number of West German Länder from ten to five or six. Yet, except for the three Länder whose territorial integrity was to be maintained (North Rhine-Westphalia, Bavaria and Baden-Württemberg), the others were adamantly opposed to the plan. As a result, after a lackluster debate a constitutional change was agreed upon between the federal government and the Länder in 1976 that turned the must-regulation on territorial restructuring (Art. 29 BL) into a mere can-rule. It has remained that way until today, as have the differences in size and economic strength among the Länder.

9 For instance, the Länder of Schleswig-Holstein and Lower Saxony were unable to shoulder reconstruction on their own, while Bavaria and Hesse would have been able to manage without help from the central government. In addition, Hamburg, Bremen and Saarland were too small to assume constitutionally mandated public tasks (*Staatsaufgaben*) of more than local proportions; by contrast, the Länder of North Rhine-Westphalia, Bavaria and Baden-Württemberg could have easily played the role of the smaller European nation states, given their population size and economic power.

10 Although not of primary concern in this study, brief reference none the less needs to be made in the field of administration to the role of local government autonomy in the German constitutional system. Despite the fact that the organization and supervision of local government clearly and indisputably belong to the legislative and organizational sphere of the Länder, the Basic Law accords an institutional guarantee to the autonomy of municipalities and counties in Art. 28. Local government bodies, which carry out large parts of the administrative function attributed to the Länder by federal legislation, thus enjoy the constitutionally status of an autonomous tier of government, which even entitles them to raise matters concerning that status before the Federal Constitutional Court (Leonardy, 1999a: 12).

11 Concurrent powers are those under which 'the Länder shall have the power to legislate as long and to the extent that the Federation has not exercised its right to legislate by Federal Act' (Art. 72 BL). Framework powers enable the federation to limit the exercise of exclusive Länder legislative functions in certain fields and to a certain extent (Art. 75 BL).

12 The Constitutional Reform Act of 27 October 1994 has altered it to a 'clause of necessity', a formulation that is supposed to favor the Länder (Leonardy, 1999a: 13). This view is supported by the fact that in the same paragraph the creation of 'uniform' living conditions has also been watered down to the goal of 'equal' ones. One might remain skeptical, however, whether in the reality of the legislative process this will amount to more than a cosmetic change.

13 The areas of shared taxes and fiscal equalization (Articles 104 to 107 BL) are the areas where the centralizing effect has been starkest. Inland revenue is divided between the Federation, the Länder and local authorities according to a mixed system of both separate and shared taxes. Shared taxes are by far the most important; of them, income and corporation taxes amount to approximately 45 per cent of inland revenues. They are shared half–half between the Federation and the Länder, in the case of income tax after a deduction of 15 per cent for local government bodies. Most important for the working of the federal system is the role of the shared value-added tax (VAT). VAT revenue is currently (since 1995) divided between the Federation and the Länder at a ratio of 56:44. This ratio is, however, not constitutionally fixed (as are income and corporation tax) but is adjusted in the light of changing financial needs approximately every two years by a Federal Act requiring Bundesrat consent (Art. 106 BL).

14 While these various measures attempt to iron out the numerous social, economic and territorial imbalances to secure 'uniform' (now 'equivalent') living conditions throughout the country as mandated in Articles 72/2 and 106/2 BL, they have come under criticism in recent years. In particular, Joint Tasks were only successful in certain areas (like university construction) but on the whole were unable to reduce regional disparities, at best preventing only the emergence of still greater differences. In addition, the close coordination between Bund and Länder caused high administrative costs and a bureaucratization of the decision-making process, both vertically and horizontally (Klatt, 1999: 44–7). Scharpf (1994) coined the term of *Politikverflechtung*, meaning an 'enmeshment' of the two levels of government. However, the problems of economic and fiscal imbalance and the necessity to act have been further compounded with the accession of the five eastern Länder in 1990.

15 Under concurrent legislative power, the Länder retain the right to legislate in a particular issue area unless the federal government does so. Hence, if the Bundesrat can block the Federation from doing so, the Länder could ensure that the federal government *de facto* could not cease the initiative.

16 Of course, this position only made sense if at first the variation in the size and efficiency of the postwar Länder, which were a result of Allied occupied zones, would be alleviated through territorial restructuring (see n.8).

17 Substates with a population between two and six million have four votes (Berlin, Brandenburg, Rhineland-Palatinate, Saxony, Saxony-Anhalt and Thuringia); those with a population between six and seven million have five votes (Hesse). Following reunification in 1990, those with more than seven million inhabitants now have six votes (Baden-Württemberg, Bavaria, Lower Saxony and North Rhine-Westphalia). Yet, no Land has less than three votes (Bremen, Hamburg, Mecklenburg-Western Pomerania and Saarland). Each Land must always cast its respective votes as a block (Art. 51/3 BL), even if it is ruled, like many Länder, by a coalition government. The now 69 Bundesrat members in total mean that 35 votes are needed for a simple and 46 for a two-thirds majority.

18 Therefore, it has been labeled, 'next to the US Senate, the most powerful second (not "upper") house in existence' (Wehling, 1989: 53).

19 In order to make compromise possible on its recommendations, its Bundesrat members (all of cabinet rank) are not subject to instructions from their Länder cabinets as they are in the Bundesrat itself.

20 The term 'reunification' is somewhat misleading, as this was not the merger of two equal partners. Technically, the German Democratic Republic 'joined' the Federal Republic of Germany according to Art. 23 BL; in other words, the GDR simply enlarged West Germany. Although a Constitutional Commission was set up to suggest constitutional alterations for the now reunified country, with the exception of token changes it merely amounted to a 'friendly take over', that is, the East adopting West Germany's constitution (still called Basic Law), legal system and political institutions.

21 Schneider (1999: 67) points out that the eastern Länder with their 20 out of 69 votes were

not awarded an equivalent veto position. Thus, future changes to the Basic Law are possible even against their unanimous opposition, which, he asserts, is a violation of the spirit of the Treaty of Unification.

22 While any discussion revolves around five 'new' eastern Länder, there are actually six because Berlin had of course not existed as a united city-state prior to reunification. Not only its geographical location but also its economic and financial situation clearly make it one of the eastern Länder.

23 Note that the Canadian federation comprises of institutions at the level of the 'whole state', the so-called First Ministers' Conference, and at the Third Level, namely the Premiers' Conference. It does *not*, however, have an institution at the 'Federal state' level similar to the role of the Bundesrat (see Chapter 4).

24 Thorlakson (2000) identifies a 'paradox' in German federalism: centralization of public finances and public goods provision on the one hand, entrenchment of Länder autonomy and distinct political communities on the other.

25 Note that fiscal federalism as an economic theory is impartial to the desirability of European integration as an end in itself. This is in contrast especially to the 'classical' political variants of integration theory in the discipline of International Relations. For the major contributions to European integration theory, see Haas (1958) for neofunctionalism; Friedrich (1969) for federalism; Moravcsik (1991) for intergovernmentalism; Pinder (1996) for new federalism; and Pierson (1996b) for historical institutionalism.

26 The Single European Act, which came into force on 1 July 1987, is a so-called framework treaty, that is, it alters and amends the Treaty of Rome through which the European Community was founded in 1957.

27 The expected benefits of the SEM were exhaustively elaborated in the officially commissioned so-called Cecchini Report on the 'costs of non-Europe', which was based on a survey of 11 000 firms and published in 1988. The report was criticized, among other things, for having given insufficient weight to the strong possibility that the benefits would be distributed very unevenly among member states, regions, and industries (Jones, 1996: 173).

28 These measures were to be enacted through the concept of 'mutual recognition', breaking with traditional arduous and time-consuming EU concept of a 'harmonization', meaning a convergence of national standards around a new European one. Sun and Pelkmans (1995), however, suggest that the resulting regulatory competition among member states, since the adoption of QMV, can be considered complementary to EU harmonization.

29 The institutional framework in the early 1980s exhibited two features. First, although the EU's supranational bodies, the Commission and the European Court of Justice, had been able to expand their influence on the Community's policies and legal structure, ultimate decisions were left to intergovernmental bargaining in the European Council (Keohane and Hoffmann, 1991; Burley and Mattli, 1993). There, in accordance with the so-called Luxembourg Compromise of 1966, the heads of state and government had to decide with unanimity, if a member state declared an issue as being of vital national importance (Moravcsik, 1991). Second, decision-making in the Council had been complicated further by the doubling of EU membership between 1973 and 1986 and the increased divergence in the level of economic development resulting from it. Four of the six new members (Ireland, Greece, Portugal and Spain) are the poorest within the Community, based on their GDP compared to the Union average. Exacerbated by ideological differences between the three largest member states (Germany, France and the UK), these factors caused stalemate in the Council and, therefore, in European integration.

30 The crucial aspect of QMV for Germany and France was that Great Britain and Denmark could not block EU social regulations in the European Council and, in turn, France, Germany and the BENELUX countries could pass any directive (see Garrett, 1992: 546).

31 Some of social regulations that were enacted as a consequence of the SEA have surpassed domestic standards even of advanced member states. Even the southern EU countries that had the most to lose from strong measures of Community regulation, as their adjustment

costs are highest, agreed to the adoption of EU directives because they were unequipped to meet the expertise of the Commission (Pierson, 1996: 153). In addition, QMV made it difficult for these member states to prevent the European Council from passing elevated regulatory standards.

32 The EU treaties have prohibited such subnational subsidies from the outset but the Commission could grant exceptions. This has changed since the mid-1980s, as the priorities of EU regional economic policies have shifted with the accession of Spain and Portugal (Müller-Brandeck-Bocquet, 1992: 170–72).

33 This is different, if domestic constitutional change is necessary, as it requires a two-thirds majority approval in the Bundesrat. Changes to the Treaty of Rome fall under this category, and the Länder used this leverage in the ratification of the Maastricht Treaty (see below).

34 As indicated earlier, this does *not* guarantee the *number* of federated units, for Art. 29 BL allows for the territorial reorganization of the country, should certain Länder wish to consolidate.

35 Note that there is no process of 'transformation' of federal legislation into Land implementation. Therefore, there is little room for maneuver in interpretation, and then only by the federal government, with regard to European directives and decisions. The Länder do not 'transform' but only execute European law (Nass, 1989: 181–2).

36 This is compounded by Art. 235 EC Treaty, which grants Brussels so-called 'implied powers'. These encompass education, broadcasting and media, that is, core Länder competencies (Gunlicks, 1994: 94).

37 The federal government reverted its initially critical position and, in the 1993 Federal-Länder Agreement, even committed itself to supporting the work of the Länder offices, in particular through its Permanent Representation in Brussels.

38 At a meeting in Bonn on 17 December 1987 the Länder Minister-Presidents established the internal Länder procedure of appointing Länder representatives based on Art. 2/5 of the Law Consenting to the Single European Act.

39 Fears outside the EU that the SEM may develop into a 'fortress Europe' have proven unsubstantiated so far. In fact, Hanson (1998) argues that the SEM, although having been developed as EU-internal trade liberalization only, brought with it the unintended consequence of external openness.

40 Like the SEA, the Maastricht Treaty is a framework treaty. This means that the provisions, which amend or alter the EC Treaty, likewise have simply been worked into the existing EC Treaty. Therefore, references to particular novelties with the TEU are made to 'EC Treaty', not 'TEU'.

41 Article J.4 states that the eventual framing of a common defence policy 'might in time lead to a common defence'. The Western European Union (WEU) is to be developed as the defence component of the Union, working in cooperation with NATO. The role of the WEU and its relations with the EU and NATO are elaborated in a declaration annexed to the Treaty.

42 The member states are required to inform and consult one another within the Council with a view to adoption of joint positions and joint action.

43 Apart from the seven titles, 17 Protocols are appended to the Treaty, which are justiciable before the ECJ. The most important of these are on social policy, operational aspects of EMU and economic and social cohesion. Furthermore, 33 Declarations are appended to, but do not form part of, the Treaty and have no legal force. They nevertheless may be used by the ECJ for interpretation (Jones, 1996: 48).

44 In general terms, the so-called Mundell-Fleming theorem posits that under conditions of capital mobility, states are faced with a trade-off between exchange rate stability and monetary autonomy; if the exchange rate is held constant, monetary policy cannot deviate from that of other countries (Frieden, 1991). Within the EU, the national room for maneuver had already been limited through the Exchange Rate Mechanism. However, its crisis in 1992/93 changed the band to 15 per cent (that is, it *de facto* gave plenty of room

for maneuver), and enabled the UK to devalue its currency and gain economic advantage as a result.

45 Although national regional policies are still operated within the Union, the governments in the less wealthy member states usually do not have the resources to tackle major regional problems by themselves.

46 The EU categorizes its regions; since July 1993, six priority objectives, that is, regions with specific attributes, exist. Objective 1 covers so-called lagging regions, usually expected to have a per capita income of less than 75 per cent of EU GDP. Objective 2 are regions in industrial decline, that is, among other criteria, unemployment rates higher than the Union average, a higher percentage of industrial employment than the Union average, and a decline in industrial jobs. Objective 3 seeks to combat long-term unemployment and to help young people and others threatened by exclusion from the labor market into work. Objective 4 is targeted at unemployment by facilitating adaptation of workers to industrial change and changes in production systems. Objective 5a is geared toward modernization and adjustment of agricultural structures, whereas Objective 5b also encompasses adaptation of fishery structures. Priority is given to developing jobs outside farming and fishing, such as tourism and small businesses. Finally, Objective 6 provides assistance to remote and sparsely populated regions in Sweden and Finland. (The European Currency Unit [ECU] was calculated as a 'basket' of the member states' currencies, relative to their economic importance within the Community. The ECU can be seen as the predecessor of the Euro, although the latter does not encompass all member states.)

47 The Edinburgh European Council decided that ECU15 billion (at 1992 prices) would be allocated to the Fund between 1993 and 1999, with 70 per cent going to Objective 1 regions. The Cohesion Fund came into existence at the end of 1993 with an annual budget of ECU1.5 billion, rising to ECU2.6 billion by 1999. It covers between 80 and 89 per cent of the costs of the projects it supports.

48 The federal government conceded this demand, and only in the concluding negotiations of the Heads of State and Government at Maastricht were the Länder excluded. In the preparation phase, the relationship of the Länder to the federal government developed in an extremely cooperative way.

49 In fiscal federalist terms, the subsidiary principle addresses public goods with purchased inputs (both pure and impure). Through it, the provision of a public good should be assigned to the jurisdiction in which the good is 'public'.

50 Each Land has one representative; the five biggest Länder send a second member. These are dominated by the executive branch; parliamentary representatives from the Länder are found only among the alternate members and the second representatives of the bigger Länder.

51 Yet, it is difficult to imagine a situation in which a Länder appeal against the Commission would be backed by the federal government, given that the Commission normally takes action only on the basis of decisions taken by the Council, that is, the member states.

52 It had been discussed in the Parliamentary Council in 1948/49 whether constitutional (that is, two-thirds) majorities should be required for transferring sovereign powers. This was explicitly rejected on the grounds that it should be deliberately made easy to transfer sovereignty. The new Europe Article has reversed the situation. If transfers alter the content of the Basic Law or make alteration possible, then a two-thirds majority in support of the measure is necessary. The simple legislative process is therefore explicitly restricted to legislating on treaty changes, which do not materially alter the Basic Law.

53 The federal government still, however, has the final say in any case in which decisions could lead to increased expenditure or reduced income for the Federation.

54 However, some controversy remains. There is no agreement on whether Bundesrat approval is also required if the federal government abstains in a Council vote where the effect is that it was not able to *prevent* the measure in question from being taken.

55 The Bundesrat has nominated about 400 representatives with regard to this point; the

effectiveness of this form of participation in any particular case will depend on how well qualified the Länder representative is to deal with the question at hand.

56 It does not matter that the Länder did not see their positions completely reflected in the final treaty. This was to be expected anyhow, since all other EU member states at the time, with the exception of Belgium, were unitary states; hence, they were not easily receptive to the demands put forth by the federal government on behalf of the Länder. Instead, what is relevant here is that the Länder clearly *did* have a significant impact on the concrete outcome of the Maastricht Treaty.

57 The major criticism of this argumentation comes from the optimal currency area (OCA) literature, which was developed mostly in the 1960s (cf. McKinnon, 1963). According to it, the EU does *not* qualify as an optimal currency area, as it is insufficiently equipped to respond to so-called asymmetric shocks. These are economic problems that originate in the difference of 'domestic' price and wage levels from those 'abroad'; the three criteria necessary to resolve them are price and wage flexibility, high labor mobility, and the availability of ample fiscal transfers from other parts of the Union. Cohen (1998: 83–4) and Jaquet (1998: 59–61) argue that the assumptions made by OCA render the approach analytically questionable.

58 The European Council, upon recommendation from the Commission, initially decided to allow 11, with Greece later 12, member states to enter the first wave of the Euro. The remaining three countries (the United Kingdom, Denmark and Sweden) have decided to remain outside the single currency zone for the time being.

Chapter 5

Implementation with a Hitch: Canada, the CUSFTA and the NAFTA

> The bottom line is that Canada's nineteenth-century division of federal and provincial powers may soon collide with the emerging global economy and the international trade agenda of the twenty-first century.
> James P. McIlroy (1997), 'NAFTA and the Canadian provinces: two ships passing in the night', *Canada-United States Law Journal*, 23: 439.

Although the so-called Fathers of Confederation established a quite centralized constitution in 1867, Canada is by now considered the most decentralized federation in the OECD world. Largely due to decisions handed down by the Judicial Committee of the Privy Council before full Canadian independence from the United Kingdom, compounded by the divide between Anglophones and Francophones, the ten provinces enjoy a degree of independent jurisdiction unmatched in other federal states. In contrast with Germany, the powers between the two orders of government are clearly divided along *vertical* lines. Federation and provinces have a set of exclusive legislative competencies for the implementation of which they are also separately responsible. Furthermore, unlike the Bundesrat, the upper chamber, the Senate, does not represent the subnational governments at the federal level.[1]

Therefore, intergovernmental relations can only be conducted *directly* between the two orders of government in so-called annual First Ministers' Conferences (FMCs) as well as regular meetings of designated ministers and senior officials in both bilateral and multilateral form. While it may occur in practice, there is no *requirement* for consensus among the provinces or among provinces and federal government built into the system.[2] The strict division of power also holds with respect to international treaties. The federal government has the authority to sign and, via Parliament, ratify international economic treaties but the latter are not self-executing. The provinces themselves have to implement those provisions that encroach upon powers under their jurisdiction.[3] This has the effect that the federal government might sign a treaty where neither it nor the other contracting parties know for certain that all aspects of the agreement will be implemented in Canada.

Corresponding to the previous chapter, the first section reveals the historical development toward decentralization and the current separation of powers. Section 2 explains how and where the bilateral free trade agreement with the United States (CUSFTA) infringed on provincial powers and how the subnational governments reacted (Stage III of the analytical framework, see Figure 3.2), as well as which role they played in the implementation procedure. On this basis, it explores the implications for both the study's null hypothesis and the fiscal federalist hypotheses outlined in Chapter 2. Finally, the topic of the third section is the North American Free Trade Agreement (NAFTA) between the United States, Canada and Mexico, which came into force in January 1994. In some respects it went beyond the CUSFTA, particularly with its side agreements on labor and the environment that had significant implications within Canada for intergovernmental relations and the domestic implementation of the side-deals. Hence, for reasons of analytical consistency and to flesh out the differences between the two treaties, section 3 mimics the second one in structure.

Canadian Federalism: Decentralization and 'Province Building'

Historical Context

The political situation in what was then British North America exhibited several cleavage lines in the mid-nineteenth century. It was made up of six colonies (British Columbia, New Brunswick, Nova Scotia, Prince Edward Island, Newfoundland and the Province of Canada – the latter two now comprising the provinces of Ontario and Québec), as well as a vast territory under the license of the Hudson's Bay Company. Each of the colonies had their own colonial government. Since frictions between the French and English colonists had already made the Province of Canada unworkable, its politicians were determined to reform the system of government. The population of central Canada was clearly in favor of a unitary state; it was seen as advantageous for developing the technical infrastructure necessary to link British Columbia to the rest of Canada.[4] However, two groups were heavily opposed to a centralized solution: first, French-speaking colonists in Lower Canada (today's Québec) feared to be relegated to minority status under such a form of government. Second, the Maritime colonies, being among the oldest British colonies with long established governments, had no intention of seeing their influence undermined in a large Dominion, dominated by the populous central Canada.[5]

Therefore, the Fathers of Confederation considered the formation of a federal union as the only reasonable option. Yet, some Canadians viewed federalism as having failed in the United States because it could not prevent the Civil War. Against this backdrop, the task for the drafters of the Canadian constitution was to limit the perceived defects of federalism and nonetheless take into account the objections of those colonists opposing a unitary state. The federal system adopted at the Québec Conference in 1864, which became known as the British North America Act 1867 and in 1982 was renamed the Constitution Act 1867 (hereafter: CA 1867), was believed to have struck this delicate balance. It gave the federal government a clear dominance of power compared to the provinces; indeed, it partly bore resemblance to a unitary system of government. The slow transformation from a very centralized system to one of the most decentralized federations in the western world was chiefly caused by interpretations of federal and provincial powers – favoring the latter – by the Judicial Committee of the Privy Council.[6]

This constitutional transition from the initial conception by the Fathers of Confederation to its present form, exacerbated by economic factors, is commonly captured in four basic periods of federal development in Canada. First, the 'quasi-federalism' from 1867 to the turn of the century is marked by the initial predominance of the national government over the provinces, with the latters' legislation frequently being disallowed by the Federation. Second, in the time of 'classical federalism' until the outbreak of the First World War the balance of power shifted to a more equal relationship between the provinces and Ottawa. During this period, various judicial decisions contributed to the steady erosion of federal powers; notably the notion of the provincial governments being subordinates of the Federation was explicitly repudiated in 1892.

Third, the 'emergency federalism' from 1914 to about 1960 saw the pendulum swing back toward the Federation. Given two world wars and the Great Depression, most provincial governments had come to the verge of bankruptcy and it became evident that only a strong federal government was capable of mastering the challenges of this period. Finally, although in the phase of 'cooperative federalism' from 1960 until the present the possibilities for provincial governments to raise revenue increased, the expectations of citizens for the provision of public services grew even faster with the development of the welfare state. For instance, health care, which falls under provincial jurisdiction, has now become one of the largest areas of public expenditure. This has led to continuous federal-provincial coordination, with the two orders of government constantly bargaining over financial resources and the frequently joint supply of public services (Malcomson and Myers, 1996: 79–81; for a slightly different categorization of the four time periods, see Whittington and Van Loon, 1996: 251–6).

The incarnation of cooperative federalism was the 'patriation' of the Canadian constitution in 1982. This meant that British authorities gave up all rights of approval of Canadian legislation. The novelties introduced with the Constitution Act 1982 (CA 1982) were twofold: first, a Charter of Rights and Freedoms was added, which continuously provokes fierce debate among policy makers and academics alike as to its benefits or misuse by certain groups. The relevant aspect for our purposes is the constitutional amendment formula contained in the Charter, requiring a minimum of seven provinces containing at least 50 per cent of the Canadian population.[7] Second, the ownership over natural resources has been added to matters under exclusive provincial jurisdiction.[8]

The continued decentralization of Canadian federalism had its most profound effect on how the separation of powers between the two levels of government has been judicially interpreted over time; it is this aspect what we turn to now.

Formal Separation of Powers

As in most federations, the separation of powers between the two orders of government in Canada is *vertical*. In other words, contrary to German horizontal and functional federalism, administrative and legislative competencies coincide, so that we only need to distinguish between the legislative and fiscal aspects within the Canadian federation. As in Chapter 3, the treaty making power will be discussed separately in the context of the first treaty that bore on it in a significant way, namely the bilateral free trade agreement with the United States.

The Distribution of Legislative Powers The powers of the Federation are mostly defined in section (sec.) 91 CA 1867, which has two parts. The first is a broad and general grant of power, giving it the authority to make laws for 'the Peace, Order, and Good Government of Canada in relation to all Matters not coming within the Classes of Subjects by this Act assigned exclusively to the Legislatures of the Provinces'. The second part of sec. 91 is an enumeration of 29 subject matters, such as 'the Public Debt and Property', 'the Regulation of Trade and Commerce' and 'the Raising of Money by any Mode or System of Taxation'. These were set down 'for greater Certainty, but not as to restrict the Generality' of the peace, order and good government (POGG) clause. Conversely, provincial competencies are largely determined in sec. 92 CA 1867. The section simply states that, within each province, 'the Legislature may exclusively make Laws in relation to Matters coming within the Classes of Subjects next herein-after enumerated'. It then proceeds to list 16 subject matters, such as 'Direct Taxation within the Province', 'Property and Civil Rights' and 'Generally all Matters of a merely local or private Nature'. Thus, it is clear that the intention was to give the federal government a comprehensive power to make law. Only certain clearly specified powers were then exempted from this general grant and given exclusively to the provinces.[9] In the same vein, the federal government's power over the legislatures of the provinces comprised the reservation and disallowance provisions. They formally vested in the central government what amounted to a federal veto, which may be applied to *any* act of a provincial legislature. These devices, again, reflect the fundamentally *centralist* character of the union as envisaged by the Fathers of Confederation.[10]

Subsequent judicial decisions, however, did not uphold this view; most of the interpretations of sections 91 and 92 by the Judicial Committee of the Privy Council relevant for our discussion involved either the opening words of sec. 91 or the trade-and-commerce power (sec. 91/2 CA 1867).

As for the former, a series of opinions *separated* the peace, order, and good government clause of sec. 91 from the 29 enumerated subheadings of that section. By 1896 the Judicial Committee held that the POGG clause gave no powers to the Federation, except when a matter was of 'unquestionably Canadian importance' and could be found neither in the enumerated subheads of sec. 91 nor in sec. 92.[11] This narrow construction was limited further when in 1923 Lord Haldane reinterpreted the POGG clause as only an emergency power, to be used in times of national crisis.

When it had become clear that the Judicial Committee of the Privy Council was willing to admit exclusive federal powers *only* for the enumerated matters in sec. 91, the federal authorities attempted to find justification for federal legislation within the various subheads of that section. The one that seemed most promising for regaining some of the legislative power lost with the narrowing of the POGG clause was sec. 91/2, 'the Regulation of Trade and Commerce'. While the Supreme Court of Canada in two early judgements in 1878 and 1880 had interpreted sec. 91/2 as an exclusive power of the Dominion, Lord Atkinson of the Privy Council reversed this interpretation in 1912. Finally, Viscount Haldane reduced the federal trade and commerce power to a 'merely ancillary' power that was only relevant 'in aid of' some *other* subhead of sec. 91.[12]

Fiscal Relations The strict vertical separation of competencies between the two levels of government, as well as the concentration of responsibilities within the Federation, is also clearly evident in the financial sphere. Because the constitution vested the legislative authority over the 'great functions of government' in the federal government, the major sources of revenue were given to the Dominion in 1867. The federal tax power as specified in sec. 91/3 CA 1867 gives the Federation the authority over 'the Raising of Money by *any* Mode or System of Taxation' (my emphasis). The provinces, on the other hand, were limited by sec. 92/2 to *direct* taxation within the province.[13]

However, through social and economic change, the major expenditure burden shifted to the provincial governments, which are in charge of the delivery of health care, education and social programs. The provinces' ability to raise revenues has not grown commensurately with the growth of their program responsibilities;[14] this resulted in two interrelated phenomena. First, *all* provinces suffered heavily when in the 1930s welfare expenditures increased by 130 per cent, with three-quarters of this burden falling upon provincial governments and municipalities. This being so, provincial revenues at the time also grew tremendously. In particular, while the costs for the traditional provincial responsibility for roads and highways grew rapidly, the coming of the automobile also brought in large additional revenues through taxes on gasoline and motor vehicle licenses. Second, there now were growing disparities *among* the provinces with more than 80 per cent of total direct-tax revenues collected in Ontario and Québec.[15] These income differences increased further with the Great Depression because tax fields such as liquor control and automobile licenses, on which provincial revenues heavily relied, tend to be very sensitive to economic fluctuations of a general nature.

With most provinces on the verge of bankruptcy, the federal government, having been denied the power to intervene directly by the Judicial Committee of the Privy Council, was forced to transfer large portions of its revenues to the provinces to help pay for their unemployment-relief programs.[16] The growth of government functions, with the vast majority of this growth at the provincial level, paved the way for the strong financial federal involvement in provincial matters through intergovernmental grants.[17] While the Federation cannot pass *laws* in areas of provincial jurisdiction, it can spend *money* on anything it wants.

The phenomena of heavily expanding subnational spending responsibilities, increased federal financial assistance and a distinction between 'have' and 'have-not' component governments is not unfamiliar from the previous chapter. However, the institutional apparatus in place in Canada through which such intergovernmental conflicts are channeled is rather distinct from the German case.

Bicameral Arrangement

Given the vertical separation of power in Canadian federalism, that is, that the provinces administer their *own* legislation, there would not seem to be a need for a provision through which the component governments participate in the enactment of federal legislation like in Germany where the Länder administer *federal* laws.

Indeed, one of the striking distinctions between German and Canadian federalism is that in discussions of the latter, the Senate as the upper chamber is rarely mentioned, neither in the academic literature nor in the media coverage. It was designed, in part, as an institution of intra-state federalism, that is, a national-level mechanism to accommodate the interests of the regions and provinces. For this reason, the 104 Senate seats are strictly allocated in numbers among the various regional parts of Canada (sec. 22 CA 1867).[18]

Contrary to popular perception as well as academic assessments,[19] the role assigned to the Senate in the constitution is a rather powerful one. To understand this, we must point out that in Canadian understanding the term 'Parliament' does not merely designate the national assembly. Instead, it encompasses three different sources of federal policymaking: first, the Queen, through her Canadian representative, the Governor General, gives royal assent to federal legislation. The House of Commons (the parliament in the narrow sense of the word) as the second component and the Senate as the third *jointly* enact federal legislation (sec. 17 CA 1867). In other words, all federal bills ultimately have to be passed in both houses to come into effect (after having received royal assent), which formally gives the Senate the power to either approve, amend, delay or even refuse government bills coming from the House of Commons.[20] However, it is extremely rare that the Senate would refuse proposed legislation; this happened only ten times in the last 50 years.[21] Should disagreement with the government majority in the House of Commons exist, the upper chamber usually tries to request an amendment.

In most cases the Senate approves federal legislation, well aware of its limited popular legitimacy as a federal institution compared to the House of Commons. This has mainly to do with the way Senators are selected; not surprisingly bearing some resemblance to the British House of Lords, Senators are political appointees with tenure until the age of 75. Depending on how many vacancies a Prime Minister can fill, s/he may be able to alter the party-political makeup of the upper house. Thus, despite its regional breakdown, the Senate has not become a forum for the expression of provincial interests. It is not seen, nor does it seem to aspire to be seen, as an organ of regional representation within the Canadian political system. Relations between the two orders of government take place exclusively *outside* the upper chamber.

Resulting Intergovernmental Relations

With the absence of a second chamber to effectively represent provincial interests, intergovernmental relations in Canada can be distinguished in two ways: first, between multilateral and bilateral contacts and, second, between political and bureaucratic ones.[22] The two most visible venues are both multilateral and political. The so-called First Ministers' Conferences (FMCs) bring together the Canadian Prime Minister with the Premiers of the ten provinces and the three territories, usually on an annual basis. FMCs have over time degenerated to events where, aware of the role the media plays in transporting the outcome to the respective constituencies, no actual negotiations take place. The second forum is the Annual Premiers' Conference (APC); as the name suggests, it encompasses the same group but excludes of the Prime Minister. APCs are held prior to the annual FMC, attempting to rally support among the provinces and set the, frequently combative, tone for the meeting with the federal government.

The second, and increasingly important, group of intergovernmental relations is bilateral, that is, between the federal and *individual* provincial governments at both the political and senior official levels; it is here where the actual negotiations take place. Similar to the German Länder, the provinces are clearly separated in terms of economic prowess. Yet, the distinction between 'have' and 'have-not' provinces is compounded by the fact that it is in part merely based on the coincidences of geography and the continued economic centrality of staples for Canada as a whole. It matters profoundly whether a province's economy is largely built on, for instance, oil and gas, forestry, grain, industrial production or fisheries. For this reason, the federal government, due to its federal spending power, primarily uses bilateral relations with the individual provinces to provide financial assistance, leading the latter to, in part, trade in exclusive provincial powers in return.[23]

The point here is that no *institutionalized* mechanism for consensus either among the provinces or between them and the federal government exists. None of the intergovernmental fora available domestically is intended to fulfill this function. Thus, various provinces are likely to have distinct positions, not exclusively but particularly, on the benefits or dangers of international economic treaties, both among each other and in relation to the federal government.[24] These differences *can*, and as we will see below on occasion indeed *do*, have the potential to compromise the Canadian negotiating position *vis-à-vis* its main trading partners. It is the impact on, and role of, the provinces regarding international economic treaties to which we now turn.

The Canada – US Free Trade Agreement: Early Provincial Concerns

Purpose and Contents of the Treaty

The traditional multilateral commitment of the United States changed at the beginning of the 1980s for two reasons: first, frustration over the slow progress in negotiations under the auspices of the General Agreement on Tariffs and Trade (GATT) had grown substantially. The issues of concern related primarily to trade restrictions in the fields of agriculture and services, as well as the protection of intellectual property rights. Second, a combination of stringent monetary and expansionary fiscal policies had resulted in an overvalued dollar and therefore a declining competitiveness in international markets. Although the ensuing use of non-tariff trade restrictions was primarily directed at Japan, these measures were of direct concern to the Canadian economy with about 80 per cent of its overall trade, around 20 per cent of Canadian GDP, conducted with its southern neighbor. Hence, the primary Canadian objective in negotiating the CUSFTA was to secure access to the US market through a binding dispute settlement process. Conversely, the United States wanted to address in a bilateral manner some of the aspects that had stalled the multilateral GATT talks at the time (McKinney, 2000: 3–5).[25] In other words, the purpose of the agreement was not free trade in the traditional sense, but the tackling of non-tariff barriers (NTBs) and market access.

Therefore, the CUSFTA is clearly not the free trade agreement that it is labeled to be. It neither achieves, nor does it seek to achieve, free trade between the United States and Canada. In fact, prior to this agreement trade between the two countries was already largely duty free, except in key sectoral areas such as textiles, steel and agriculture. The average tariff on Canadian exports to the United States was approximately one per cent; nearly 80 per cent of Canadian trade with the USA was already duty free. In addition, the existing trade restrictions in agriculture, steel and textiles remained largely untouched in the CUSFTA (Whalley, 1992: 133). The agreement nonetheless contains a commitment to eliminate remaining bilateral tariffs over a ten-year period.

The CUSFTA consists of 21, partly rather complex, chapters and as such it is longer than the GATT. The topics covered range from agriculture, wine and spirits, energy, autos and government procurement to services, finance and dispute settlement procedures; among them are what have been termed 'empty chapters', that is, lengthy treatments with limited substance, especially the chapters on agriculture and government procurement.[26] Three issue areas of the CUSFTA stand out as novelties:

First, Chapters XIV to XVII move beyond mere trade in goods by introducing the new topics of services, travel of businesspersons, investment and financial services. It was in essence agreed to treat each other's providers like domestic ones,[27] although Chapter XIV on services contains few substantive provisions, as all existing service arrangements in both countries are 'grandfathered'.[28] Second, Chapters XVIII and XIX establish an institutional basis for the settlement of disputes between the two countries. While the former applies rules and regulations to the treaty as whole, the latter specifically deals with trade remedy measures, reflecting the Canadian concern with US anti-dumping and countervailing duties, aimed at growing bilateral disputes, especially over softwood lumber trade.[29] Yet, contrary to Canada's objective, both countries actually *retain* their respective laws, that is, the United States can continue to employ anti-dumping and countervailing measures. What is new, however, is that the disputes *themselves* are no longer a matter of national law; instead, the CUSFTA replaces domestic judicial review procedures with a bilateral one. This means, for instance, that Canadians sit on panels which ascertain whether or not US law was properly followed, as well as if changes to US legislation are consonant with GATT and CUSFTA provisions (Hart, 1992: 28).

Third, several aspects of the agreement were of particular importance to the Canadian provinces, particularly agriculture (Ch. VII), wine and distilled spirits (Ch. VIII) and government procurement (Ch. XIII); we explore their impact next.

Encroachment on Provincial Competencies

Several chapters of the CUSFTA had the potential to intrude upon the powers of the component governments, since the respective provincial policies could be seen as *de facto* NTBs. Among these are agricultural marketing boards (Ch. VII), provincial and municipal government procurement (Ch. XIII) and, in particular, provincial regulation of wine and distilled spirits (Ch. VIII). At issue in the latter was the pricing policy, i.e. the practice of provincial liquor boards of imposing a tax on non-domestic alcoholic beverages. Under the CUSFTA, US liquor would have to be treated like Canadian brands. As this had been a trade irritant between the two countries for a long time, a separate chapter within the CUSFTA was devoted to it. Beyond these three areas, there was the question of regional development policy, which is explicitly allowed under GATT. It is the chief means of 'province building', and includes among its instruments subsidies, loan guarantees, grants and tax provisions, i.e. precisely the kind of NTBs that the CUSFTA wanted to curb. Minimally, it was expected that the agreement would mandate an alteration of the means of provincial industrial policies admissible, moving away from direct assistance toward an emphasis on technical infrastructure and a skilled labor force (Simeon, 1988: 206–7).[30]

It must be stressed that the CUSFTA negotiations presented the *potential* for these intrusions into areas under provincial jurisdiction. Since the provinces were not briefed about the 'last minute "brinkmanship"' (Brown, 1988: 89) between the Canadian and US negotiators, part of the *Elements of the Agreement* released on 4 October 1987 took the component governments by surprise. The final text of the CUSFTA, which was released two months later, had an extremely limited direct impact on matters under provincial jurisdiction. Subnational procurement in both countries has been exempted from Chapter XIII – although it is stated in the chapter that the intention is to *eventually* extend the agreement to all levels of government (Calvert, 1988: 132). Provincial technical barriers (Ch. VI) were excluded as well, while provincial regulations pertaining to the services (Ch. XIV) and investment (Ch. XVI) chapters were 'grandfathered'; the postponement of subsidies for a second phase equally obviated immediate provincial impact. It was *only* Chapter VIII (wine and distilled spirits) that required instant provincial implementation (Anonymous, 1988: 44).

This being said, what mattered at the outset of the bilateral free trade negotiations for both orders of government was that there was significant *potential* that powers under provincial jurisdiction could be intruded upon. Once the 'Elements' were concluded, the immediate political context of October 1987 still dictated that the federal government needed the support of a least a majority of the provinces (Brown, 1988: 90). As we will see in what follows, their approach *during* the negotiations was based on the potential for encroachment and their reaction once the CUSFTA was *signed* on their constitutional clout.

Stage III: Provincial Reaction and Effect on Treaty

The Canadian constitution is unique in distinguishing between the *making* of international trade treaties and their *implementation*. The former clearly falls within the federal realm under the regulation of trade and commerce of sec. 91/2 CA 1867.[31] Until Canada gained full legal independence from Great Britain in the late 1920s, sec. 132 CA 1867 vested the authority in Parliament to introduce federal implementing legislation, provided the international agreement in question was an Empire treaty. Since Canada began entering into treaties as a legal person in its own right, sec. 132 CA 1867 no longer applies. Instead, the Judicial Committee of the Privy Council under Lord

Atkin ruled in the so-called Labor Conventions case in 1937 that the federal government's power to sign an international treaty does *not* extend to the implementation of provisions that domestically fall under provincial jurisdiction.[32]

In other words, in the implementation of international treaties the domestic separation of powers embodied in sections 91 and 92 CA 1867 applies: the federal government can only enforce agreements in areas of its own jurisdiction. In sharp contrast to other federations, international treaties do not automatically become the law of the land in Canada but may require implementing legislation. If the non-conforming regulations in question fall under provincial authority, then it is up to the individual provinces to enact legislation. 'This is the sense in which there is indeed a "provincial veto"' (Simeon, 1988: 191).[33]

As mentioned above, before and during the CUSFTA negotiations, there was every reason for both orders of government to believe that the final agreement would significantly touch upon powers under provincial jurisdiction. The so-called Macdonald Commission had expressed this expectation most clearly in its 1985 report. Officially labeled the 'Royal Commission on the Economic Union and Development Prospects for Canada', it strongly recommended initiating negotiations with the United States for a comprehensive bilateral free trade agreement. Advocating a 'comprehensive' treaty, the Commission therefore expected that, among other areas, provincial subsidies, procurement practices and liquor board policies would be covered by any such deal. On this basis, given the constitutional separation of powers, it advised close consultations between the two orders of government about each other's objectives *prior* to the negotiations, as well as a binding commitment to accomplish them. *During* the bilateral trade talks, provincial representatives should be in attendance to counsel the federal delegation if needed. This would also enable the former to be closely informed about the ongoing negotiations with the United States at all times (Brown, 1988: 80).

Almost all provinces had endorsed the Macdonald Commission's proposal for bilateral free trade negotiations – and its proposal for close provincial involvement in the development of the Canadian position.[34] To determine how this should be instituted, at the Halifax FMC in November 1985 Prime Minister Mulroney endorsed the 'principle of full provincial participation' in the upcoming bilateral trade talks with the United States. As could have been expected, considerable disagreement arose subsequently between the two orders of government about the concrete meaning of 'full' provincial participation, especially since the actual trade negotiations did not commence until June 1986. The Prime Minister had, just prior to the FMC in Halifax, appointed Simon Reisman, who was known for his adversarial attitude toward the provinces, as Canada's chief negotiator. Conversely, Alberta's Premier Don Getty argued in a letter that the provinces' view on 'full' participation meant the overall negotiating mandate was to be established by the FMC and designated ministers, *not* the federal cabinet.

A compromise was forged between the First Ministers in June 1986, stating that they would meet every three months during the negotiations to review the progress, and designated ministers would meet as required. Furthermore, chief negotiator Reisman would be responsible *only* to the federal cabinet, and *no* provincial representatives were to be part of any bilateral negotiating sessions. Reisman's mandate was to be established by the federal government, but *in consultation* with the First Ministers and designated ministers. Close ongoing deliberations to provide liaison and advice was to be established through a senior committee of federal and provincial officials, called the Continuing Committee on Trade Negotiations (CCTN), chaired by Simon Reisman. Finally, the federal government would formally seek the *views* of all provinces prior to signing any agreement. Yet, a determination of the provincial role in the implementation of the agreement was notably absent from the compromise (Brown, 1988: 81–3).

While during the bilateral trade negotiations from June 1986 to August 1987 the CCTN was indeed the center for the exchange of views and information, federal and provincial administrators disagree on its effectiveness. Federal officials maintain that the CCTN often was privy to the first elaboration on the Canadian negotiating position, even before the federal cabinet, and this with a far greater degree of detail and confidence than even the business community.[35] The provinces indeed used this venue to advance issues of particular sensitivity to their jurisdictions; for instance, they all sought various exemptions and copious transition periods in the chapter on agriculture (Simeon, 1988: 196). Provincial feedback in the Committee also enabled the Canadian negotiators to confront the United States with broad subnational backing, where possible. This was of importance, as the Americans repeatedly maintained the need for assurances of provincial implementation (Anonymous, 1988: 43). On the other hand, provincial representatives in the CCTN complained that not only were they hardly able to review hard copies of actual negotiating texts or proposals, but also meetings often degenerated to mere federal slide presentations. Further, the negotiators only 'heard' those provincial concerns that would fit the predetermined federal negotiating position (Doern and Tomlin, 1991: 132–3).

However, even this limited and one-sided degree of information sharing on the part of Simon Reisman and his team began to vanish when the Ontario Liberal government was reelected in September 1987. Premier Peterson, who had fought his campaign on an anti-CUSFTA platform, publicly voiced his reservation against parts of the proposed trade agreement. Manitoba's Premier Pawley joined him in expressing his doubts in the press (Doern and Tomlin, 1991: 148).

> The federal negotiators began, it would appear, to take this as a signal that full provincial consensus would almost certainly not be forthcoming. It can be assumed that scenarios for an agreement which minimized direct encroachment for provincial jurisdiction were reviewed with increased emphasis from this stage onwards (Brown, 1988: 88–9).

The open expression of such provincial veto power in the final stages of the CUSFTA negotiations clearly alarmed both the Canadian and American negotiators and likely prompted the exact formulation of the 'federal state' clause in Art. 103 CUSFTA; it states that the federal governments would 'take all necessary measures to ensure provincial and state compliance with the articles of the Free Trade Agreement' (Delagran, 1992: 24).

Stage IV: Implementation of the CUSFTA

For the immediate bilateral free trade negotiations, the Macdonald Commission had recommended close consultation by the federal government with the provinces in the *hope* that this process would create enough political pressure on the latter to implement particular CUSFTA provisions as required (Simeon, 1988: 201).[36] Nonetheless, given the intractable constitutional separation of powers, '[i]t was clearly in the federal government's interest to portray the CUSFTA as "99 per cent in federal jurisdiction", to downplay the opposition in certain provinces' (Brown, 1988: 89), especially because of US concerns about provincial compliance. After it had become clear that provincial unanimity in support of the CUSFTA was unattainable, subnational support in line with the constitutional amendment formula, that is, at least seven provinces comprising a minimum of 50 per cent of the Canadian population (sec. 38/1b CA 1982), developed as the target.[37]

In the end, this goal, which requires the inclusion of either Ontario or Québec as by far the most populous provinces, were indeed in favor of the CUSFTA, as Premiers Pawley of Manitoba and Ghiz of Prince Edward Island joined Ontario's Premier Peterson in opposition to the agreement. Yet, the Ontario government had objected to the CUSFTA most rigidly, in particular because of the federal decision to remove duty-remission programs from the 1965 bilateral Auto Pact in order to conclude the Chapter X negotiations on trade in automotive goods. The province had been consulted prior to the federal decision but did not provide constructive input (Doern and Tomlin, 1991: 149).

It turned out that *only* the CUSFTA's provisions on alcoholic beverages (Chapter XIII) mandated an *immediate* alteration of provincial practices in their liquor board policies. Beyond this, the agreement's impact on *current* provincial government policies was mitigated in two ways. First, stipulations in those chapters of the CUSFTA where existing provincial regulations could be challenged by the United States (chiefly, but not exclusively, Chapters VII, IX, XIII and XIV on agriculture, energy, government procurement and services, respectively) were 'grandfathered'. This means that provincial measures already in place *prior* to the implementation of the CUSFTA on 1 January 1989 were exempt from coverage. In other words, most of the agreement's burden was imposed on *future* provincial governments; they will be constrained in their choice of policy instruments, since any *new* regulation must be consistent with the CUSFTA.

Second, Ottawa's approach to implementing legislation was designed to offer as small a target to provincial government objections and a potential subsequent constitutional challenge as was feasible. It had initially entertained three possible courses of action of which the least *immediately* obtrusive was chosen after consultations with provincial governments indicated that the support of some was contingent on adopting a 'minimalist' approach (Anonymous, 1988: 45). Since the vast majority of the CUSFTA fell under federal jurisdiction, the implementing Bill C-130, introduced in spring 1988, was largely devoted to making the necessary changes to existing federal legislation. Two clauses are devoted to provincial implementation. Clause 6 affirms that Parliament reserved the right 'to enact legislation to implement any provision of the Agreement or fulfill any of the obligations of the Government of Canada under the Agreement'. Although the legal effect of this statement, because of provincial jurisdiction, is limited, it is intended first and foremost as a warning against non-complying subnational governments (Robinson, 1993: 207). Clause 9 is devoted directly to wine and distilled spirits (Chapter VIII CUSFTA). It authorizes the federal government, following consultations with the province(s) in question, to introduce regulations and impose penalties, if it considered such measures necessary to give effect to Chapter VIII in one or more component units (Delagran, 1992: 27).

The main purpose of this 'implementation package' lay in the balancing act between avoiding immediate provincial confrontation by 'grandfathering' most of the provisions in question, and the obligation of Art. 103 CUSFTA to take 'all necessary measures' to ensure provincial compliance.[38] In this sense, Bill C-130 was also a message to the United States about the federal government's commitment to 'deliver' its subunits (Anonymous, 1988: 47; for an insider's account of the formulation and tabling of the Bill in the House of Commons, see Ritchie, 1997: 157–76).

Implications for the Null Hypothesis and the Fiscal Federalist Hypotheses

To recall, the study's null hypothesis posits that extant domestic institutions did *not* mediate in the concrete form the CUSFTA took. We can say that they mattered at least insofar as the provinces for the first time had obtained a regular consultation procedure with the federal government during the negotiations that they were determined to enhance in future trade treaty negotiations (Doern and Tomlin, 1991: 150). Yet, the provinces themselves complained that their representatives often merely 'received' information from Simon Reisman and his team, rather than being able to actively participate in developing the federal negotiating position; hence, no *direct* and *immediate* impact of the provinces on the CUSFTA could be proven. This being said, the provinces made it known in the FMC and the CCTN talks that they were adamant to have certain sectors and policy areas within their jurisdiction exempted from the bilateral trade agreement (Dunn, 1988;

Simeon, 1988: 196). *All* these demands were reflected in the final Agreement; on the surface, this would suggest that at least *indirectly* the provinces themselves were successful in having their concerns incorporated in the agreement.

However, the federal negotiators incorporated only those provincial propositions that coincided with their own view (Delagran, 1992: 21). It was more likely the constitutional impasse, that is, the potential veto power of the individual provinces in the implementation procedure, rather than provincial input during the negotiations *per se* that had the federal government 'volunteer' to severely limit the encroachment on its subunits (Brown, 1988: 89; Delagran, 1992: 25). In either case, the impact of the domestic institutional framework was clearly visible both in the actual treaty provisions (or better, exemptions thereof), as well as in the subsequent domestic implementation procedure. A rejection of the null hypothesis would be consonant with Garrett and Lange's expectation that the obstacles to advancing policy change, namely a comprehensive trade treaty, increase with the number of institutional veto players.

Regarding the fiscal federalist propositions, none of the three public sector functions have been supranationalized with the CUSFTA. Some would find this startling, given the high degree of economic interdependence between the two countries (cf. Mattli, 1999: 179–88). While more than three-quarters of Canadian foreign trade depend on the USA, Canada is, with about 40 per cent, also the United States' largest trading partner; it would have seemed to justify the supranationalization of at least *some* regulatory public goods. Against the backdrop of this *asymmetrical* economic relationship, one might point to the relative strength of the United States *vis-à-vis* Canada, its lesser degree of dependence being a reflection of a domestic market almost ten times the size of its northern neighbor. After all, it was Canada that proposed the negotiation of a bilateral trade agreement in order to secure its economic access to this market at a time when protectionist rhetoric was widespread in US policy.

However, *both* sides had *no* intention to move beyond a mere trade agreement. This has little to do with the US's power but a lot with a distinction in 'political culture' between North American and continental European countries in terms of the role of the 'state' in the 'market' (see Chapter 3). These differing conceptions are mirrored in regional integration schemes; it is here where fiscal federalism appears deficient.

NAFTA and Its Side-Agreements: Trying to Avoid Provincial Obstruction

Purpose and Contents of the Treaty

When negotiations for the NAFTA commenced in June 1991, the goals of the three countries were quite diverse. The initial proposal to negotiate a free trade agreement with the United States had come from the Mexican government under President Salinas a year earlier; after having introduced neoliberal economic reforms, Mexico was in dire need of foreign direct investment. Its dependence upon the US market very much mirrored the Canadian situation. The United States had primarily three objectives. It wanted to lock in neoliberal reforms in Mexico and was attracted by the prospect of freer access to its 90 million consumers. Most importantly, the Americans aimed for a liberalization of the country's investment rules to take further advantage of Mexico's low labor costs in their competition with European and Japanese rivals (Shoch, 2000: 122). Canada was not interested at the start to join the negotiations, as it had already concluded the CUSFTA and had no significant commercial ties with Mexico. Nonetheless, fears of a so-called hub-and-spoke system grew, where only the United States had largely uninhibited access to both markets.[39] Therefore, Canada joined the talks solely for defensive purposes, eager to avoid a 'reopening', that is, watering down, of *any* part of the CUSFTA in the trilateral negotiations (see Cameron and Tomlin, 2000: ch. 4).

Unlike the bilateral agreement, NAFTA consists of two parts: the commercial NAFTA, and the side agreements on labor (NAALC) and the environment (NAAEC). The latter were negotiated after the commercial NAFTA had already been concluded.[40] In general terms, the 22 chapters, along with several annexes, of the commercial treaty largely represent a continuation of the CUSFTA, albeit with a number of departures, and its extension to Mexico.[41] The basic rules laid out in Chapters III to V, especially tariffs and content rules, stipulate that the former are to be eliminated completely between the members by 2008, but with transition periods for a variety of 'sensitive' sectors in the three countries of between five and 15 years. Only products with at least 60 per cent North American content qualify for duty-free shipment; the automotive sector now mandates a 62.5 per cent national content, compared to 50 per cent in the CUSFTA.[42]

The three parties agreed not to conclude a trilateral agreement on agriculture (Chapter VII), given the parallel negotiations in the Uruguay Round of the GATT where the United States and the EU were in a stand-off. Therefore, the CUSFTA provisions were carried over, while the US and Mexico negotiated separate tariff reductions that were also encompassed in Chapter VII. The agreements on government procurement, investment and services (Chapters X to XII) departed from the CUSFTA to a greater extent. The federal entities and sectors covered by the procurement chapter were expanded, now also including services, and setting new monetary thresholds above which government purchases are open for competition. One of the new aspects in the investment chapter is that subnational governments have been included in the prohibition to employ investment-related performance requirements as trade barriers.[43] Finally, a significant semantic alteration was instituted in the services chapter insofar as it now applies to all service providers save those that are clearly mentioned as exempted, whereas the respective CUSFTA chapter worked on the opposite principle, i.e. a commercial service had to be explicitly *in*cluded.[44]

New in NAFTA is not only a treatment of intellectual property (Chapter XVII), but also Chapter XV on competition policy. The latter originated in Canada's failed attempt during the CUSFTA negotiations to remove the US's resort to trade remedy laws, i.e. anti-dumping and countervailing duties, for secure market access.[45] Although the Canadian negotiators could not convince the United States to replace anti-dumping rules with an NAFTA-wide competition policy, Chapter XV did establish some limited obligations for the operation of state enterprises (Cameron and Tomlin, 2000: 33–50).[46]

In the subsequent negotiation of the side agreements on labor (NAALC) and the environment (NAAEC) which were completed on 13 August 1993 unions and environmentalists had hoped that newly elected President Clinton would press for the adoption of NAFTA-wide internationally binding standards (Mayer, 1998: 168–9; see also Rupert, 1995). These hopes were quickly dashed, as the United States settled for the 'domestic enforcement of domestic laws', leaving the regulatory discrepancies with Mexico unchanged.[47] To monitor adherence to the enforcement requirements, two commissions were set up, each consisting of a ministerial council (cabinet-level representatives from the three countries) and a permanent secretariat for technical and administrative assistance to the council. In case of a 'persistent pattern of failure to effectively enforce' a domestic law covered by the side agreements, an arbitration panel could in the extreme impose financial penalties (see McKinney, 2000).

Encroachment on Provincial Competencies

A number of provisions of the commercial agreement apply to subnational governments as well: for instance NAFTA's new investor-state dispute process for enforcing private property rights can be used to challenge not only federal but also provincial measures (Robinson, 1993: 207). This being said, separate from the main text but nonetheless part of the commercial NAFTA are seven annexes that declare exemptions from the treaty *as a whole*, since they are not associated with any specific chapter. Annex I encompasses policies and entire sectors, like social services, that the signatories exclude from the NAFTA. 'States and provinces have up to two years after the agreement's entry into force to identify *any* other reservations they wish to add to Annex 1' (Lipsey *et al.*, 1994: 66; my emphasis).[48] This does not qualify the fact that *future* policy options of provincial governments are severely constrained, as any changes in provincial legislation *after* the NAFTA came into force on 1 January 1994 must comply with NAFTA regulations.

The more immediate concern appeared to come from the side agreements, given that environmental and especially labor legislation fall clearly within provincial jurisdiction. The risk that a financial penalty might be imposed under either one of the side agreements is remote, for it is unconceivable that a provincial government would *deliberately* avoid enforcing its *own* environmental and labor regulations. However, *if* an arbitration panel were to detect a 'persistent pattern of failure to effectively enforce' a domestic laws covered by the agreements, it could levy fines of up to US$20 million against either level of government.[49]

Stage III: Provincial Reaction and Effect on Treaty

In striking difference to the CUSFTA negotiations, the involvement of the provinces during the NAFTA talks received hardly any public, let alone academic, attention.[50] This may chiefly be due to the fact that the future consultation of the provinces was seen as having been firmly established with the CUSFTA (Doern and Tomlin, 1991: 150). In addition, the multilateral negotiations in the Uruguay Round of the GATT, in which the provinces were engaged as well (see Chapter 6), reached its final and critical stages simultaneously with the NAFTA talks.

Similar to the CUSFTA procedure, the provinces demanded 'full participation', and the two orders of government agreed to institute a separate federal-provincial committee of senior officials modeled after the CCTN particularly for the trilateral trade talks, the C-NAFTA (Committee for the North American Free Trade Agreement). It met ten times during the course of 1991, with the actual commercial negotiations between the three countries only commencing on 12 June. The atmosphere in the C-NAFTA was decidedly different from the CUSFTA experience, which in no small measure had to do with the choice of Canada's chief negotiator for the NAFTA talks. John Weekes, selected from the trade ministry and previously Canada's ambassador to the GATT negotiations in Geneva, unlike Simon Reisman, was known for his very collegial style (Cameron and Tomlin, 2000: 9). The provinces this time were privy to all federal draft texts before they were tabled in the trade negotiations and considered their participation, short of being 'in the room' of the NAFTA negotiations, as 'full' as was imaginable. Provincial representatives were also directly involved in the Canadian delegation for the final negotiations on the NAALC and NAAEC, which were signed by the contracting parties on 14 September 1993.[51]

Stage IV: Implementation of NAFTA

The federal strategy for the implementation of the commercial part of the NAFTA was in some ways similar to that of the bilateral free trade agreement five years earlier. First, the immediate encroachment on provincial jurisdiction was minimized through the 'laundry list' of Annex I that ultimately led to an exemption of all existing subnational non-conforming laws in the three signatory states. Yet, contrary to the CUSFTA experience, limiting the agreement's impact on the provinces was not a one-sided reaction by the federal government to the prospect of judicial conflict and its reputation *vis-à-vis* the US negotiators. Instead, the measure was coordinated with the provinces, reflecting the altered federal-provincial quality of consultation during the NAFTA negotiations. This does not change the fact that several chapters of the commercial NAFTA, like the CUSFTA, pose considerable legal constraints on the policy instruments that *future* provincial governments can utilize, as these then have to conform to NAFTA provisions.[52]

Second, Art. 105 NAFTA is identical to Art. 103 of the CUSFTA; it stipulates that the signatory parties employ 'all necessary measures' to ensure compliance of their component governments with the agreement. This can be interpreted as a 'whatever it takes' formulation, as otherwise the member states in both trade treaties could have settled for the less stringent GATT formulation (Robinson, 1993: 211). Yet, Art. 105 NAFTA does not mandate judicial action on the part of the federal government. It is up to its discretion to utilize, for instance, the federal spending power to 'persuade' provinces in question to obey NAFTA regulations within its jurisdictions – it would likely be a less time-consuming and more effective means, compared to a drawn-out court battle.[53]

The above rationale, however, does not apply to the side agreements. Since environmental regulations are significantly, and labor rules almost exclusively, within provincial jurisdiction, the provinces made it known to the federal government that it must not invoke the 'federal state' clause of Art. 105 NAFTA for the NAAEC and NAALC, so as not to insinuate to the US and Mexican governments that the matters covered in the side agreements were under federal jurisdiction.[54] Instead, the two levels of government negotiated intergovernmental agreements that, on the basis of Annexes 46/4 NAALC and 41/4 NAAEC regulate the participation of those provinces that opt-in to be covered, in the dispute settlement procedures should they occur.[55] The Canadian Intergovernmental Agreement (CIA) on the NAALC was signed in May 1995 by the federal government and Alberta; so far, the provinces of Manitoba (January 1997), Québec (February 1997) and Prince Edward Island (October 1998) followed. The federal and Alberta governments signed the CIA regarding the NAFTA's environmental side agreement in August 1995; subsequently Québec in December 1996 and Manitoba in January 1997 opted-in as well.[56]

The implications of the NAFTA side agreements – and the subsequent intergovernmental agreements in Canada[57] – are twofold. First, they alter the veto player concept (see Chapter 3) by effectively giving each *individual* province a veto power, as they cannot block the side agreements directly but indirectly. By not opting-in, they not only prevent them from applying in their *own* jurisdiction but can also ensure that the NAALC and NAAEC do not apply in Canada as a whole, given the 55 per cent thresholds in terms of labor force and GDP, respectively. Second, the very exemptions for the Canada in the side agreements, *de facto* avoiding employment of the, compared to the GATT, more forceful 'federal state' clause in the commercial NAFTA, are a reflection of the potential difficulties the country's political system faces in international trade negotiations. The United States has repeatedly demanded assurances of provincial implementation in Canada (Anonymous, 1988: 43; Delagran, 1992: 26). These concerns were also voiced in the multilateral trade negotiations under the auspices of the GATT, primarily by the EU (Schaefer, 1997: 464), which will be explored in the last chapter.

Implications for the Null Hypothesis and the Fiscal Federalist Hypotheses

As during the CUSFTA negotiations, provinces were lobbying for exemptions of particular sectors and policy areas under their jurisdiction from the commercial NAFTA; a general immunity of all provincial regulations in existence prior to the agreement's coming into force was indeed granted in Annex 1 of the NAFTA. However, like the previous bilateral case, this does not mean that *direct* provincial influence on the federal negotiators could be proven as having been responsible, despite the significantly improved federal-provincial consultation process during the negotiations. The federal government itself had an interest in instituting Annex 1 to avoid the risk of subsequent confrontation over implementation – and the concomitant criticism of its trading partners. In contrast to the US states, the provinces were informed well ahead and could complete the initially required lists of non-conforming subnational regulations on time. In this sense, the null hypothesis can be rejected; the domestic institution of competitive federalism *did* influence provisions of the treaty – like the impact of the Bundesrat could only come to bear by virtue of its constitutional role.

The side agreements explicitly encompass separate rules for their application in Canada (Annexes 46 NAALC and 41 NAAEC), denoting the federal inability of treaty enforcement in areas primarily under provincial jurisdiction. They entail opt-in provisions for the individual provinces and the 'federal state' clause of the commercial NAFTA (Art. 105) does not apply, which translated into the new constitutional terrain of federal-provincial CIAs. Even clearer than in the commercial NAFTA did the constitutional framework shape the side agreements, as they do not ultimately cater to component governments in all three countries (like Annex I above) but to implementation in the Canadian provinces specifically. The null hypothesis can be rejected here as well.

As for the fiscal federalist hypotheses, neither the commercial NAFTA nor the side agreements result in the supranationalization of any public sector functions.[58] In contrast to the bilateral free trade agreement, however, they do establish a limited number of common institutions. The Free Trade Commission (FTC), formally NAFTA's governing body to oversee the agreement's implementation, consists of meetings of the three designated ministers, which '... seem to be held mainly because the NAFTA agreement calls for them to take place at least once a year' (McKinney, 2000: 238). This being said, the FTC also has a number of subsidiary working groups. Turning to the side agreements, the Commission for Labor Cooperation, together with its national offices, conducts studies of and provides information on labor conditions in North America but the institutional structure established with the NAALC does not allow for remedial action in the case of proven labor abuses. By contrast, the Commission for Environmental Cooperation is more developed, having its own secretariat to carry out and administer scientific analyses and adjudicate complaints of failure to enforce domestic environmental standards.

Yet, all three institutions are of an intergovernmental, not a supranational nature. The side agreements themselves are limited to the domestic enforcement of domestic laws; no NAFTA-wide regulatory standards were established. As with the bilateral free trade agreement, the point here is not the asymmetrical distribution of economic and political power within NAFTA, which far exceeds the imbalances between member states of the EU. None of the three signatory states envisioned an EU-type regulatory framework – and the proposed Free Trade Agreement of the Americas (FTAA) speaks to difference in 'political culture', that is, the role of 'the state' in 'the market' that Fiscal Federalism appears to neglect.[59]

In summation, the assessment of institutional adaptation is consistent with the propositions by Garrett and Lange (1996) – and Fiscal Federalism – as we expect bigger difficulties the more decentralized a political system is, that is, the higher the number of institutional veto players. Although we rejected the null hypothesis for both parts of the NAFTA, the concrete adjustment was decidedly different than in centralized Germany. They focused on explicit treaty exemptions – rather than incorporation – 'grandfathering' to delay the immediate impact on component governments and granting the individual provinces veto player status – rather than a second chamber collectively. The institutional 'adaptation' to trade treaties, although they display a far lower degree of integration than their European counterparts, none the less has to concentrate on conflict avoidance due to the decentralized Canadian constitutional framework.

It is precisely these differences in the degree of institutionalization between the two macro-regions which are addressed in the concluding chapter, to which we now turn.

Notes

1 Instead, having been modeled after the British House of Lords, its members are appointed by the Prime Minister, albeit according to a constitutionally mandated regional formula (see below).

2 Differences of opinion are justified with either economic or cultural heterogeneity among the provinces, or both. As we have seen in the previous chapter, the former exists in Germany as well. The latter is immaterial here in so far as I am concerned with international *economic* treaties only. Yet, the cultural distinction between the predominantly French-speaking province of Québec and the English-speaking 'rest' is relevant to a certain extent for the *form* federalism in Canada has taken.

3 In this sense, the Canadian federation is distinct within the OECD world. Not only Germany, but also the United States, Australia, Austria and Switzerland do not need to involve their subunits in the implementation of treaties signed by the federal government.

4 An added advantage was that it could thereby also serve to prevent the United States from expanding further north, as well as allowing for the number of British troops and personnel necessary to administer the colonies to be reduced.

5 'From the very beginning, Canada was confronted with two serious political divisions: the split between French and English, and a division between centre and periphery' (Malcomson and Myers, 1996: 76).

6 Whittington and Van Loon (1996: 203) point out that this is technically not a court at all. It is made up of judges who are appointed to the Queen's Privy Council in Britain and who are mandated to advise the monarch on the disposition of appeals from the common-law courts. The Judicial Committee was responsible for ensuring that the laws enacted by the colonial legislatures were not repugnant to the laws of Britain. Because the BNA Act was a British statute, the Judicial Committee had to ensure that the laws passed by the provincial legislatures and the Parliament of Canada were consistent with its provisions.

7 Two additional events aptly represent the era of cooperative federalism. The Meech Lake (1987) and Charlottetown (1992) accords were attempts by the federal government to resolve the continued tensions over Québec's place in the federation that had loomed at least since the beginning of the 1960s. Both accords were designed to grant the predominantly French-speaking province more powers but ultimately failed to achieve precisely the minimum threshold of the new constitutional amendment formula.

8 This must seen against the background of the so-called National Energy Program (NEP), conceived in 1980 by then Canadian Prime Mister Trudeau. In the wake of the second oil crisis, it mandated that the oil producing western provinces, mainly Alberta, had to sell within Canada under the world market price in order to supply the manufacturing industries in central Canada with sufficient cheap resources and thereby boost the economy. It led in western Canada to what became known as 'western alienation' (from central Canada at large, and the capital Ottawa in particular). The NEP was discarded one year later, but it had caused enough resentment for the provinces to fiercely demand that natural resources within their borders be brought under their jurisdiction.

9 There are a few additional provisions within CA 1867, such as education (sec. 93) which, although within exclusive provincial jurisdiction, gives the federal government the responsibility to protect the education rights of religious minorities from encroachment by the provinces. Sec. 95 establishes concurrent federal-provincial powers for agriculture and immigration. While both levels of government may enact laws in these two areas, it institutes federal paramountcy in case of conflicting provisions between federal and provincial laws. Finally, sec. 109 grants the provinces full title to 'all Lands, Minerals, and Royalties' within their boundaries, a concession that was not viewed as very important in the pre-petroleum era. Yet, this control over crown land, and therefore over both renewable and non-renewable natural resources, has become a major source of provincial power since the Second World War.

10 The reservation provision gives the lieutenant governor of a province the power to reserve a bill for the 'pleasure of the Governor General in Council', after which, if no positive action is taken by the federal official, the bill dies. In the case of the disallowance power, the federal government can unilaterally invalidate any provincial law within a year of its passage. Both powers were used extensively before the turn of the century, and then intermittently in the 1940s, when the last disallowance was recorded. Although still part of the constitution, by convention they have become vestigial appendages in a federal system that has become decentralized to an extent that such heavy-handed centralist devices are no longer acceptable (Whittington and Van Loon, 1996: 197–9).

11 In other words, the Federation was granted exclusive jurisdiction *only* for matters that

came under one of the *enumerated* subheads of sec. 91, discarding the general grant of federal authority at the beginning of sec. 91, which is what the drafters of the constitution had in mind.

12 The possibility to appeal decisions of the Supreme Court of Canada at the Judicial Committee of the Privy Council was abolished in 1949; yet, the constitutional ground rules of Canadian federalism were quite firmly established by 1925.

13 Direct taxes include personal income tax, corporate income tax, real property tax and inheritance tax. The courts have tended to emphasize the *intention* of a provincial tax measure as the crucial determinant of its validity, rather than limiting it if incidental *effects* might be indirect. The clearest example is the retail sales tax, which is a very important provincial revenue source today; here the provinces have been able to collect revenue from the retailer, which is in fact passed on to the customer through a legal fiction. The retailer is assumed to be the *agent* of the government for the purposes of administering this tax. By deeming each retailer a provincial tax collector, and by requiring that the tax be calculated separately from the before-tax price, the sales tax can technically pass as a direct tax on the consumer. *If* the sales tax were instead to be included in the prices of retail goods (a much simpler arrangement for all concerned and used in Europe with the VAT) and collected from the store, it would be *indirect*. The retailer would be 'indemnifying himself at the expense of the customer' by increasing the retail price of the goods.

14 In the 'fiscal blueprint' of 1867, government was expected to confine itself mainly to the provision of national security, the administration of justice and promoting national economic development through big projects such as railways. Thus, at the time of Confederation, the most important and costly functions were placed in the hands of the federal government. The provinces, by contrast, were to take on matters of a merely 'local or private nature' such as education, public welfare and public woks within the province. Since these powers were of minor importance at the time, provinces were anticipated to require only limited sources of revenue.

15 The cause of this inequity was the growing number of national companies with head offices in Toronto and Montreal. Provincial corporation taxes were (and still are) imposed at the head office of a corporation – profits earned by corporations across the country were taxed almost exclusively by the governments of Ontario and Québec. This has been an important factor in the serious regional disparities in provincial revenues to the present day (Whittington and Van Loon, 1996: 283–4).

16 One major response to the fiscal crisis was the appointment, in 1937, of the Royal Commission on Dominion-Provincial Relations (the so-called Rowell-Sirois Commission), which was charged with reexamining the economic and fiscal basis of Confederation and of the distribution of legislative powers, given the changes in the previous seven decades. In its report delivered in 1940, the Commission recommended an extensive shift of both governmental functions and tax powers, the latter involving a permanent system of unconditional federal equalization payments to needy provinces and a fully integrated tax system. Yet, the outbreak of the Second World War effectively preempted an action on the Rowell-Sirois recommendations.

17 Three large groups of federal transfers have been established in the postwar period. First, the so-called Canada Assistance Plan (CAP), instituted in 1966, provides matching federal grants to help the provinces pay for social assistance. Since there is no upper limit to the amount of the transfer to each province and they negotiate bilaterally the outlines of a proposed program with the federal government, the distribution of the CAP transfers varies a great deal from province to province. Second, the most popular government program continues to be shared-cost-social program *medicare*, incepted in 1967. It provides for a 50 per cent federal funding of the overall national costs of almost all physicians' services. Third, the so-called Established Programs Financing (EPF) was designed to replace the older cost-sharing arrangements for provincial health-care programs and for post-secondary education (PSE) with a combination of more tax room

for the provinces and a block-funding formula. The amounts involved are by far the largest of the intergovernmental transfers. While the PSE component is unconditional, the federal government passed the *Canada Health Act* in 1984 to place strict conditions on EPF health transfers, prohibiting provinces to allow doctors to 'extra-bill' their patients (Whittington and Van Loon, 1996: 291–6).

18 The two most populous provinces, Ontario and Québec, the three Maritime provinces (Nova Scotia, New Brunswick and Prince Edward Island) and the four Western provinces (Manitoba, Saskatchewan, Alberta and British Columbia) each receive 24 seats. In addition, Newfoundland, which only entered the Canadian federation in 1949, is entitled to six Senators, whereas one senator each represents the Yukon and Northwest Territories. When the Northwest Territory was split in 1999 to create Canada's third territory, named Nunavut, the number of Senators increased to 105. In contrast to the provinces, the territories are not constitutionally independent from the Federation.

19 Tsebelis (1995), in his examination of bicameral systems, dismisses the function of the Canadian Senate as lacking the *constitutional* clout to act as an institutional veto player in federal decision-making – contrary, for instance, to the German Bundesrat and the US Senate (cf. Chapter 3).

20 Nonetheless, federal legislation can be introduced in *either* chamber (although the government proposes the vast majority of bills in the House of Commons), and both go through three readings with intermittent delegation to standing committees.

21 The most politicized event in recent years was the temporary refusal of the Senate, the majority belonging to the Liberal Party at the time, to pass the bilateral free trade agreement with the United States that the conservative government under then Prime Minster Mulroney had negotiated. When Mulroney called fresh elections and turned out to be victorious, the non-elected Senate took the popular vote as a clear sign to drop its resistance and passed the CUSFTA (see below).

22 In recent years, an additional layer has been added, namely the coordination with the Aboriginal population that, in a number of cases, has been granted the status of 'nations'. Coordination with them does complicate the intergovernmental picture; yet, it does not have a bearing on the present investigation.

23 This particularly holds true for the have-not provinces of Atlantic Canada, which are heavily dependent upon federal funding. Conversely, the more affluent and powerful provinces of Alberta, Québec and Ontario have acquired the manpower and expertise to be a match for the federal staff. In other words, the negotiating power among the provinces is very unequal, allowing the economic disparities to thrive through the federal spending power and ensuing bilateral intergovernmental relations.

24 The distinction from Germany is instructive here. Similarly distinct economic variation among the Länder has *not* prevented a unified position of the subunits on macro-regional integration, notwithstanding possible disagreements in *domestic* politics; conflicts with federal views could also be reconciled in a timely and cooperative manner. The institutional condition that ensures this *modus operandi* is the role of Bundesrat in federal legislation, which requires broad Länder consensus as well reconciliation with the federal government (cf. Chapter 4).

25 By contrast, Lusztig and James (1996) doubt that the Canadian government at the time had an interest in the CUSFTA *per se*. They charge that then Prime Minster Mulroney was primarily committed to resolving the long-standing constitutional dispute about the role of the French-speaking province of Québec in what became known as the Meech Lake Accord – which ultimately failed. Only in order to ensure support for this scheme from the free-trade oriented provinces in Western Canada did Mulroney embark on the free trade negotiations with the United States.

26 The agreement was concluded in a last minute marathon session on 3 October 1987, was signed by Prime Minister Mulroney and President Reagan on 2 January 1988 and, after a long and heated ratification debate in Canada (see below), finally went into effect on 1 January 1989.

27 This is *different* from employing joint regulations. Hence, while Chapters 14 to 17 appear to resemble the four freedoms instituted with the SEA, the CUSFTA is based on the GATT's national treatment rule (ch. V CUSFTA) as opposed to the common market's 'mutual recognition'. The latter concept allows all goods and services to be offered in the host country as long as they abide by the regulations of their *home* market, whereas the former focuses on the regulations of the *host* country. This means that US service companies doing business in Canada will now be treated according to Canadian law (Rugman, 1994: 111).

28 'Grandfathering' denotes the practice of conflict avoidance by not dealing with the thorny issue of provincial implementation until a particular provincial practice is actually challenged under the CUSFTA. In other words, there is no *immediate* need for implementation by a component government.

29 Anti-dumping and countervailing trade policies are defensive measures invoked by the US government, frequently at the request of particular sectors. The intent is to fend off advantages that Canadian companies allegedly gain through the adoption of various schemes that in essence allow them to sell their goods and services at a lower price abroad than at home.

30 Since the CUSFTA did not establish any bilateral institutions to oversee adherence to its provisions, the potential intrusion could only be *directly* on the basis of the provinces' domestically guaranteed powers. Note the difference from the additional *indirect* threat of EU decision-making for the Länder competencies.

31 Delagran (1992: 17) points out that Canadian treaty law does *not* require Parliament to give consent to the ratification of an international agreement. Rather, it has merely become constitutional convention for the federal government to table treaties in the House of Commons and the Senate for approval.

32 The case emanated through Canada's membership in the International Labor Organization, which had adopted three conventions that mandated its member countries to pass laws on minimum wages, weekly working hours and rest time. The federal government's attempt to enact the legislation was struck down, since most labor laws fall under provincial jurisdiction. Lord Atkin charged that it otherwise would open a panacea for federal intrusion into provincial competencies. As he put it: '[Even though] the ship of state now sails on larger ventures and into foreign waters, she still retains the watertight compartments' (McIlroy, 1997: 434).

33 However, since the current practice is founded on judicial interpretation, the constitutional separation of powers with respect to international treaties is not clear-cut. The dispute revolves around whether the federal trade and commerce powers, as well as the residual POGG clause in the opening of sec. 91 CA 1867, could be expanded to cover most if not all elements of legislation needed for implementing trade treaties. The question has not been tested in the courts yet, but it would amount to a reversal of the much-criticized ruling in the Labor Conventions case. This legal uncertainty, as much as the existing separation of powers on treaty making, influenced the federal-provincial consultations during the CUSFTA negotiations (Anonymous, 1988: 42–3).

34 At the APC in Newfoundland in August 1985, Ontario's newly elected Premier David Peterson was alone in questioning the necessity for a free trade agreement. For lack of formal unanimity, the Premiers took no vote on the subject; yet, even Ontario did not openly oppose the idea at the time (Brown, 1988: 79).

35 Not all provinces could give CCTN discussions the same degree of attention. The larger provinces had well established bureaucracies and appointed full-time trade representatives solely responsible for the negotiations. The smaller provinces, by contrast, not able to shoulder the costs of such a commitment, chose senior officials from within their existing structures. Thus, on many issues, if Ontario, Québec and Alberta took differing views, most other provinces simply echoed the position of one or the other of the lead provinces (Brown, 1988: 86–7).

36 For the longer term, the Commission had outlined three alternatives to *de facto* enhance

the federal power in the implementation of international trade treaties. First, the federal government could assume the power to implement all such agreements, including those that partly infringe on provincial jurisdiction. Second, and only slightly more realistic, Senate membership could be based on elections with clear regional delineation; the second chamber would then have to *ratify* international trade treaties before the federal government can introduce its implementing legislation. The third option is that Parliament ratifies international agreements, as well as, if necessary, enough provincial legislatures to match the constitutional amendment formula, after which point the treaty is self-executing (Simeon, 1988: 200–201).

37 Strictly speaking, the section refers to 'at least fifty percent of the population of the provinces', which means that the three territories do not count. However, their small number of inhabitants could not influence the population threshold of the amendment formula anyhow.

38 The emphasis on 'all *necessary* measures' was meant to tighten the commitment of this 'federal state' clause compared to Art. XXIV(12) of the original GATT agreement in 1947; the latter required each contracting party to take 'such *reasonable* measures as may be *available* to it' (my emphases).

39 This would create an incentive for Canadian businesses to relocate to the United States. In this context, an agreement without Canada also bore the risk that Mexico might be able to negotiate an even better access to the US market than Canada had achieved under the terms of the CUSFTA.

40 The commercial negotiations were completed in August 1992, at the height of the US presidential election campaign, in which Clinton as eventual successor to Bush positioned himself as willing to conclude NAFTA only if separate agreements on labor and the environment were negotiated. The move was intended to distance himself from the incumbent without rejecting NAFTA altogether, while trying to satisfy enough Democrats sympathetic to labor and environmental interests to eventually win Congressional approval if elected president.

41 Indeed, one of the major challenges of the NAFTA was to forge an agreement of two G8 members, whose economic interaction was already based on the CUSFTA, with a nation whose business practices and lagging legal framework still exhibited some features of a less developed country.

42 Rules of origin are crucial for free trade areas, since the member states gradually remove tariffs and non-tariff barriers between each other, but they retain their different duties and quotas for trade with non-members. For instance, if Canada has a lower external tariff on a particular product than the United States, non-NAFTA products could be imported via Canada and then be sold within NAFTA. To avoid this, the content requirements are always a bone of contention in free trade areas. Customs unions like the EU, which have a *common* external tariff, by definition, need not concern themselves with this topic.

43 Also relevant in this context is the new so-called investor-state arbitration, which enables foreign investors to take complaints about a NAFTA party to an international arbitration body *themselves*, rather than having to go via their national government.

44 This principled change was consequential for the negotiation of exemptions, for Canada most importantly in the cultural industries. In the words of one Canadian negotiator: 'So the question is, how do you get the status quo where the rules work differently?' (quoted in Cameron and Tomlin, 2000: 228). Within the NAFTA services chapter, telecommunications and financial services were explicitly excluded – and covered separately in Chapters XIII and XIV – as was government procurement (Chapter X).

45 The United States argued in the CUSFTA talks, as it did in the NAFTA negotiations, that the abolition of its trade remedy laws necessitated a change of domestic legislation that the President had no chance of getting past a partly protectionist Congress.

46 The dispute settlement proper is outlined in Chapters XIX and XX. The latter applies to the NAFTA as a whole, sets up a system of panels with national nominees, a NAFTA secretariat as well as a Free Trade Commission, comprised of cabinet ministers, as an

oversight body. Chapter XIX mainly mirrors its CUSFTA predecessor, having binational panels determine on a binding basis whether the imposition of anti-dumping and countervailing measures correctly apply the domestic law of the country in question, and whether legislative changes are consistent with NAFTA provisions.

47 Furthermore, mainly on the insistence of Canada, the environmental side agreement does not apply to provisions governing the management of the 'commercial harvest or exploitation, or subsistence or aboriginal harvesting, of natural resources' (Robinson, 1993: 202–3). On the labor side, dispute resolution was introduced for the enforcement of child labor and minimum wage laws, while industrial relations, that is, the right to organize and strike, were exempted on insistence of Mexican business (Mayer, 1998: 202).

48 This amounted to an exemption of *all* existing subnational legislation that was in clear or potential violation of the NAFTA at the time – provided they were identified as such by the respective component government. The provinces had prior notice of this measure through their constant consultation with the Canadian negotiators; thus, they were able to complete their lists well ahead of the deadline. Yet, the US states had not received early information and subsequently informed the federal government that they were unable to sift through their state laws to identify non-conforming state legislation, demanding the US government do it for them. As a result, the three contracting parties agreed upon American request that *all* existing subnational legislation not consistent with the NAFTA is now *automatically* exempted. The detailed provincial lists had been compiled to no avail (correspondence with Helmut Mach, Executive Director for Trade Policy, Alberta Department of International and Intergovernmental Relations).

49 In contrast to European environmental regulations, the environmental side agreement does not aim at limiting pollution but rather treats the environment as a competitiveness issue (Beukel, 1999: 124–5).

50 A notable exception is an article by Abelson and Lusztig (1996), in which they trace the decision of the Ontario government under Premier Rae to first endorse but ultimately oppose the NAFTA agreement. Yet, the authors' aim is primarily to advance the explanatory capacity of their rational choice model.

51 This assessment is based on correspondence on 22 November 2001 with Helmut Mach, Executive Director for Trade Policy, Alberta Department of International and Intergovernmental Relations.

52 Annex 1 is in essence an NAFTA-wide 'grandfathering' arrangement. However, when the ratification bill passed in the House of Commons on 27 May 1993 and in the Senate on 23 June, all NAFTA provisions, again, were 'grandfathered'. As with the CUSFTA, the latter implies a federal claim to enforcement.

53 Since the Canadian Federation is the signatory to international trade treaties, any charge of non-compliance on the part of another party will be directed to the federal government, even if the violation is caused by new legislation in one or more of the provinces.

54 Note, however, that the side agreements do *not* require provincial governments to alter their laws or regulations. Even without individual provincial opt-ins, the side deals merely create a long and convoluted dispute resolution process at the end of which the federal government is liable unless and until it is able to convince a non-complying provincial government to improve the enforcement of its own laws.

55 To that end, both intergovernmental agreements establish two commissions, one by the respective designated ministers, the other consisting of senior officials from the federal, provincial *and* territorial governments. The latter are treated as part of the federal government's jurisdiction in the side agreements.

56 All other provinces have indicated that they have no intention to sign the environmental intergovernmental accord. The reasoning is based on the *potential* financial penalties of up to US$20 million for non-enforcement. They are a deterrent because, due a mistake by the federal government in the NAAEC negotiations, penalties are computed on the basis of the *Canadian* (rather than provincial) GDP; this would clearly bankrupt any of the

have-not provinces. The provinces that *did* opt in have done so due to the unlikelihood that penalties would be imposed; they also signed the side agreements as part of the 'package'.

57 Both intergovernmental agreements grant the provinces the lead role in disputes involving their enforcement practices (Articles 7/6 [labor] and 7/3 [environment]). Yet, the legal standing of such agreements is still unclear, for they have not been tested in the courts yet (Schaefer, 1997: 484).

58 Since 2003, an academic as well as public debate has ensued in Canada about whether or not to deepen bilateral integration with the United States; proposals concentrate either on a sectoral customs union or a single currency (see Hülsemeyer, forthcoming).

59 'Of course NAFTA aimed for a much lower level of economic integration, with no harmonization of external tariffs, economic policies, or social policies, so a less elaborate institutional structure was required. Also, the countries of North America desired to avoid what was perceived to be an overly bureaucratic institutional framework in Western Europe' (McKinney, 2000: 238).

Chapter 6

Conclusion: Federalism as an Obstacle?

> I sense that what has already happened with the United States and with discussions with the E.U. on GATT procurement is that the next time we all shuffle to the table and sit down, the E.U. is going to tell Canada, then maybe they should not be sitting at the table because everyone is there to talk about subunits, and Canada does not have much of a track record in delivering their subunits, so maybe they should sit out this session. I do not think we are there yet, but I do see a pattern emerging.
>
> James P. McIlroy, quoted in Matthew Schaefer (1997), 'Searching for Pareto gains in the relationship between free trade and federalism: revisiting the NAFTA, eyeing the FTAA', *Canada-United States Law Journal*, 23: 492.

The study has traced the ratification and/or implementation processes of regional economic treaties in Germany and Canada, as well as the role of subnational governments in the negotiation of these preferential trade agreements. The purpose was to determine how varied federal constitutions, explicating both the *extent* and the *form* in which component governments can act as institutional veto players, thereby influence the institutional adjustment to the trade treaties that are a state response to globalization.

The Theoretical Argument

To recapitulate, Chapter 2 reviewed Cerny's argument about the constant adjustment pressure of states to economic globalization and the subsequent inevitable demise of the welfare state and its replacement by what he terms the 'competition state' (1995). Two questions arose: first, if 'the state' indeed were no longer capable of providing the public goods it used to, where would they be shifted? I showed that European MNCs were not so much interested in domestic competition but rather an EU-wide regulatory framework with certain social underpinnings. This being so, I pointed to the neglect of the institutional variation among the two 'successful' integration schemes (Mattli, 1999), the EU and NAFTA. It suggested an exploration of the conditions that determine the reassignment of PSFs in one region but not the other.

This coincided with the second aspect of Cerny's argument that required clarification. His thesis of 'changing political economies of scale' logically implied that their assignment could be clearly determined to begin with, that is, *prior* to globalization. I held that the analysis could profit from the economic sub-discipline of Fiscal Federalism, which is concerned about the welfare-optimal assignment of public sector functions among various levels of government (Oates, 1977). Extrapolating its logic beyond the domestic realm for which it was originally conceived, I generated three hypotheses about the conditions under which the supranationalization of certain PSFs would seem to be welfare-optimal. Irrespective of their empirical merit, any propositions based on the tenets of Fiscal Federalism take on a normative form, that is, they propound what governments *should* be doing to accomplish the welfare-optimum, and they are *outcome*-oriented, downplaying political factors.

To analytically account for these limitations, Chapter 3 proposed tracing the process of institutional adaptation in a comparative case study, given the considerable differences. I outlined the analytical model by Garrett and Lange (1996) which emphasizes two sets of domestic institutions that the authors assert mediate between altered societal preferences according to economic globalization (Frieden and Rogowski, 1996) and the actual policy change instituted by the national government. While the organization of the labor market between employers and unions as either more neo-corporatist or pluralist reflects 'societal institutions', the authors subsume the political regime type and the codification of electoral formulae, institutional veto players and bureaucratic independence under the rubric of 'formal public institutions'. I argued that four of the five categories could be either held constant or neglected in a comparison between Germany and Canada, isolating the notion of so-called institutional veto players. It denotes the *constitutionally guaranteed* power of those actors legitimized by a subnational constituency to effectively block any policy change. It follows that the more decentralized a political system is, that is, the more institutional VPs it has, the less likely 'political entrepreneurs' can overcome these vested interests to alter the *status quo*.

Three aspects of Garrett and Lange's model required clarification for our purposes. First, while they take the change in societal preferences due to globalization and its direction as given, I pointed to differences in 'political culture' between continental European and North American economic and political actors, drawing on the sociological concept of morphogenetic cycles (Archer, 1996). This variance reflects contrasting ideas about the proper role of 'the state' in 'the market' and comes to bear in the different degrees of institutionalization between the EU and NAFTA. Second, according to Tsebelis (1995), the power of second chambers in bicameral systems is the only criterion to determine the number of institutional VPs. With a view to the comparison between the German and Canadian federations, I submitted that the concept needs to be broadened to account for *other* constitutional provisions that pertain to the power of component governments in federal systems. This is imperative for *international* economic treaties that touch subnational powers; otherwise, it leads to inaccurate predictions about the prospects for policy change. Tsebelis's argument was developed for *domestic* political decisions, for which its validity is undisputed.[1]

Third, even when the differences in the number of institutional VPs *among* federations are thereby taken into consideration, the concept is none the less based on the premise that the constitutional rules in federal systems are unambiguous and clearly distinct from unitary ones. After probing into the 'murky waters' of the literature on federalism, as the distinction of unitary systems in part is less clear-cut than is commonly believed (Duchacek, 1970), I developed the analytical framework for the empirical investigation of this study, integrating the above theoretical insights (Figure 3.2). It conceptualizes two access points for subnational governments as the institutional VPs in federal systems. While they are crucial for the ratification and/or implementation procedure of PTAs that encroach upon competencies under their jurisdiction, they also may have an influence on the negotiating position of their respective federal governments before the trade treaty in question is signed. Depending upon the concrete ratification and/or implementation, it may result in a feedback loop; put differently, the veto power of component governments in future treaty negotiations is altered (usually enhanced).

Empirical Evidence

The 'unitary federalism' of the German federation covered in Chapter 4 is marked by an unusual functional and horizontal separation of powers between the two orders of government, reflected in the strong role of the Bundesrat in federal legislation and constitutional amendments. The decision-making rules require broad consensus *among* the Länder in the Bundesrat as well as *between* federal government and second chamber. This became evident in the ratification procedures for the Single European Act and especially the Maastricht Treaty. The SEA Ratification Law, to the development of which the federal government consented voluntarily as the constitutional necessity was not beyond doubt, and the constitutional changes in connection with the Maastricht Treaty were both negotiated in a short period of time. Concerning the latter, with the new Art. 23 BL as well as the extension of Art. 50 BL the Länder agreed to have their interests regarding EU matters represented *collectively* through the Bundesrat in areas that domestically fall under their individual jurisdiction, continuing the practice of centralized decision-making. By the same token, these constitutional changes almost amount to an extension of the Bundesrat's function in domestic politics to the EU realm.

Chapter 5 recorded a rather different experience in the Canadian case. While the German federation was marked by an increased centralization of decision-making over time, the opposite occurred in Canada. Although conceived by the Fathers of Confederation with a high degree of centralization of powers in the federal government, subsequent 'imaginative' interpretations of the constitution by the Judicial Committee of the Privy Council have turned the Canadian federation into the most decentralized one among OECD countries. This extends to the implementation of international treaties, which are not self-executing once ratified but require separate provincial legislation for treaty provisions that encroach upon their legislative powers. Since the wide-ranging competencies of the provinces are not channeled through a regional chamber equivalent to the Bundesrat, there is no institutional mechanism to force a measure of consensus among the provinces or between federal and provincial governments.

The first consequence for the implementation of both the CUSFTA and the commercial NAFTA was the participation of the provinces in the development of the Canadian negotiating strategy. While the federal government dominated the process during the CUSFTA talks, it improved substantially during the NAFTA negotiations, partly due to the different styles of the Canadian chief negotiators.[2] The second implication, given the constitutional impasse, was a strategy of conflict avoidance by the federal government when it turned out that even the consultation of the provinces during the negotiations could not alleviate provincial obstruction on largely ideological grounds, particularly on the part of Ontario. The elements utilized by the federal government comprised of crafting treaty language that limited provincial incursions (CUSFTA), the 'grandfathering' of all existing non-conforming provincial laws in the federal implementing legislation (CUSFTA and NAFTA) and invoking the 'federal state' clause. The latter was more stringently formulated in the CUSFTA and NAFTA compared to the GATT but due to 'grandfathering' in the main did not apply immediately either.

The approach in the NAFTA side agreements on labor and the environment had to be different, for both fell largely under provincial jurisdiction. The NAALC and NAAEC already contained annexes specifically catered to the Canadian political system, allowing the provinces to opt-in, that is, to be bound by the side deals. Complemented by the subsequent intergovernmental agreements between federal and provincial governments on the domestic implementation, they effectively gave the *individual* component governments veto player status. Consequently, the NAALC has been signed by only four provinces so far (the last in 1998), the NAALC by three (the last in 1997).

Findings

The Null Hypothesis

The null hypothesis, that extant domestic institutions would *not* have any impact on the treaty outcome, could be rejected for both countries, albeit to varying degrees and with quite different implications. The weakest case was the ratification of the Single European Act in Germany, as it was constitutionally not beyond doubt that the Bundesrat *could* oppose the treaty – notwithstanding the fact that it had no intention to do so. The federal government therefore *agreed* to a Bundesrat ratification law, which in the tradition of German federalism marked its collective style. Yet, the Bundesrat had no (positive) influence on the SEA as such. The situation was different with the Maastricht Treaty, where the necessity of Bundesrat approval was beyond doubt. The federal government negotiated three of the four initial Länder demands in the TEU, namely a regional chamber, the principle of subsidiarity and representation of the Federal Republic through a Bundesrat representative in case of exclusive Länder competencies being at stake in Brussels. The Treaty itself and especially the subsequent ratification procedure further strengthened the Bundesrat position in EU matters, being the clearest case of a feedback loop (cf. Figure 3.2).

Conversely, in *both* the CUSFTA and the NAFTA the provinces' influence on the treaties in question was clearly visible, however in a different *form* than under the German constitution. In the CUSFTA, once it became obvious that unanimous provincial support was not forthcoming, the Canadian government engaged in crafting treaty language that would minimize subnational encroachment. In its implementing legislation, it further 'grandfathered' all existing non-conforming regulations to delay any potential conflict even further. In the commercial NAFTA treaty, a general exemption of all existing subnational legislation was written directly into Annex 1 of the treaty, again reinforced through the 'grandfathering' clause in the federal implementing bill. The NAFTA side agreements even have particular provisions for their application in Canada, allowing the *individual* provinces to decide whether or not they wish to be bound, effectively allowing them not only to avoid their application in their own jurisdiction but also, at least the populous provinces, to prevent the *other* provinces, in conjunction with the Canadian government, from reaching the thresholds set out in the side deals. (For a schematic depiction of the study's findings for the null hypothesis and the fiscal federalist hypotheses, see Table 6.1.)

These discoveries are largely consistent with the expectations about the degree of centralization of political systems, but with one qualification. Canada as the decentralized federation may still be implementing the trade treaty in question at the federal level. However, this is achieved only through conflict delay with the provinces and – equally as important – at the cost of suspicion and pressure from Canada's main trading partners. In other words, the constitutional test of a challenge of provincial legislation under either one of the trade treaties is still pending.

Fiscal Federalist Hypotheses

In the German case, the fiscal federalist hypotheses generated in Chapter 2 have been, with the exception of fiscal policy, successful in explaining the

Table 6.1 Schematic Findings

	SEA	TEU	FTA	NAFTA
Null Hypothesis (*no* influence of constitution trade treaty)	✔/✘ (unclear subnational effect)	✘ ('positive' subnational effect)	✘ ('negative' subnational effect)	✘ ('negative' subnational effect)
Fiscal Federalism: Hypothesis 1 (stabilization)	n/a	✔ (except fiscal policy)	✘	✘
Hypothesis 2 (distribution)	✔ (*regional* redistribution)	✔ (*regional* redistribution)	✘	✘
Hypothesis 3 (allocation)	✔	n/a	✘	✘

✘ Rejection
✔ Confirmation

supranationalization of public sector functions to the EU. With the SEA, regulatory policies covering all economic activity were moved to the macro-regional level (Hypothesis 3). The Maastricht Treaty subsequently also shifted collective redistributive (Hypothesis 2) and monetary policies (Hypothesis 1) to Brussels. I submitted that their supranationalization with the TEU was a consequence of the previous shifting of regulatory public goods in the wake of the SEA.

By contrast, no supranationalization of PSFs occurred in either of the regional trade treaties signed by Canada. One would typically point to the dominant position of the United States within North America, insinuating that, given its large domestic market, it had no urgency to give up powers to a supranational entity, in which its influence would sink relative to the current situation. No economy within the EU has comparable clout. While this statement of course cannot be disputed, I maintain that it is not relevant for the present discussion, that is, an explanation of the institutional variance between regional integration treaties. Instead, the point here is that *neither* member of the CUSFTA and NAFTA had any intention to embark on an EU-type path. I hold that this therefore cannot be explained by differences in economic and political power, but by distinctly different conceptions of the degree to which 'the state' should regulate 'the market'. I have suggested that the differences between continental European and North American countries in this respect are necessarily reflected in the kinds of PTAs the respective member states sign. It is here where Fiscal Federalism could benefit from a consideration of the constitutional and political circumstances under which its predictions are advanced.[3]

Hence, of the two scenarios outlined in the first chapter, namely that either federalism as a state form is an obstacle at large, or that the degree of centralization is also decisive among federations, this study lends itself to support the second scenario. The number of subnational veto players does indeed matter, but we must take into account constitutional provisions beyond the role of second chambers, if the regulations in question have a direct bearing on the leverage of subnational governments as institutional VPs. I do not suggest that the Canadian federation did not adapt to the PTAs it signed, but at question was the 'flexibility' (Boeckelman, 1996: 9) with which this took place. While the German system could tackle the far-reaching encroachments on Länder powers directly and swiftly through constitutional amendments, the Canadian strategy has been one of postponing the contentious aspects through 'grandfathering' provisions for the time being; the constitutional 'test' still remains to be taken. In addition, the side agreements do *not* require the provinces to change any legislation or to adopt new labor and environmental standards. Despite having signed PTAs that do not reassign any public sector functions, uncertain implementation puts a strain on Canada's position *vis-à-vis* its main trading partners.

The Uruguay Round of the GATT: Same Treaty, Different Process

Caveat and Counterfactual

As pointed out in the discussion of different political cultures about the desired state's role in the economy, the two PTAs discussed above vary considerably in the 'extent of commercial preferences granted to members' and the range of non-trade related issues covered (Mansfield and Milner, 1999: 616).[4] The Maastricht Treaty encompasses a whole array of policy areas and was written to achieve economic, institutional and social purposes. It, therefore, includes regulatory, distributive and redistributive provisions that had to be ratified as a 'single undertaking', to use the WTO phrase – despite the initial opt-out clauses for Denmark and the United Kingdom. By contrast, the CUSFTA and the NAFTA are narrow and, even with respect to the side agreements, employ only minimal 'regulatory' instruments. Clearly, most provinces must see it as such, given that their lack of support, particularly of the NAAEC, is rooted in concerns over potential financial penalties. In other words, a broad comprehensive treaty might expand the winset for policy change, while a narrow treaty may limit it. If so, then it would be possible that the treaty *type* could have an independent effect, not accounted for in this analysis. The likelihood of this being the case can be examined through a counterfactual. How would the German federation have dealt with a side agreement-like treaty, and how would Canadian provinces have reacted if the NAAEC had been a mere chapter *within* the commercial NAFTA? In Germany, the issues covered in the NAFTA side agreements would fall under federal jurisdiction to begin with (although an agreement that does *not* establish common standards is most unlikely in the EU). In the Canadian case, one can speculate whether the provinces would have been less likely to refuse to implement the side agreements if they had endangered the NAFTA as a whole. However, even within the commercial treaty there are different strategies to exempt subnational units from NAFTA obligations (see Schaefer, 1997).

The second option to 'control' the institutional variation in PTAs is to consider a multinational trade treaty that was been signed by *both* countries. Such an instance was the Uruguay Round of the GATT; it stretched from 1986 to 1993, that is, it took place simultaneously with the negotiation of the four regional integration schemes under consideration here. The reason for these time-consuming talks had to do with the number of issue areas that were on the GATT agenda for the first time: trade-related intellectual property, trade-related investment measures and services. While all three eventually resulted in separate agreements, the single area that on several occasions threatened to derail the entire round was agriculture. Precisely because of its contentiousness it had been avoided in the previous seven GATT rounds. Although the severe differences between the United States and the EU dominated the debate, the subsequent brief discussion will solely focus on the part of the German Länder and Canadian provinces, or their absence, in these negotiations.[5]

If the role of subnational governments is broadly consistent with the findings of Chapters 4 and 5, then the institutional differences between the macro-regional integration schemes are negligible, whereas the variation of domestic constitutional frameworks would be confirmed as decisive instead.

Canada and Germany: Provinces versus EU

Canada is a member of the so-called Cairns group, which comprises 14 agricultural exporters (incl. Australia and New Zealand) that are committed to the promotion of free trade in the sector. This being said, the Canadian position within the Cairns group became severely compromised during the Uruguay Round because there were, and are, significant import-sensitive producer groups within Canadian agriculture, exhibiting clear regional cleavages (Chapman, 1996: 8; Hart, 1998: 177). The grain-exporting Western provinces of Alberta, Saskatchewan and Manitoba were decidedly in favor of lifting all non-tariff barriers, since they export beyond the (actually also highly subsidized) US market. Conversely, Canada has extreme import protection for dairy, poultry and eggs, which are concentrated in the two by far most populous provinces, Ontario and Québec. In general, farm production in central Canada and the Atlantic provinces is much more subject to provincial marketing boards and support programs than is the case in the prairie provinces (Brown, 1989: 225). When the then Director-General of the GATT, Arthur Dunkel, released a draft treaty to restart the agricultural negotiations in December 1991 (the so-called Dunkel Draft), it proposed a 'tariffication' of import quotas, which affected Canadian lobby groups argued would decimate the number of farmers in these supply-managed sectors.

In mid-December, the 117 contracting parties were supposed to initial the Uruguay Round agreement in Geneva, to be signed in April 1994 by the designated ministers in Morocco. Since the Geneva talks were not scheduled as a ministerial meeting, the federal government had not invited the Canadian provinces. (The component governments *do* receive an invitation from the federal government to attend – at their own expense – if ministers of the contracting parties meet.) The provinces of Alberta and Québec, the starkest free trade and supply management advocates, respectively, nonetheless decided to send representatives to Geneva. Much to the dismay of the federal negotiators, both lobbied them until the last moment, Québec not to sign the agreement, Alberta to do so. Given that Ontario and Québec elect two-thirds of all members of parliament, Canadian negotiators rejected the 'tariffication' of agricultural sectors against all other trading partners, which in the end included even Japan. When it became clear that the Round would be concluded without Canada, the negotiators on the final day were forced to reverse course and adopt Alberta's position.[6] On 15 December 1993 the agreement, which largely followed the Dunkel Draft, was initialed. Import quotas would be converted to their tariff equivalents and reduced over six years by a minimum of 15 per cent per item.[7]

By contrast, no German Länder had been involved in any form in the Uruguay Round talks – neither was the German government for that matter, since trade negotiations had been delegated to the EU. While the member states initially agree on the common position, EU representatives lead the discussions and sign international trade treaties. Their legal enforcement is certain, as EU law takes precedence over national law. The epigraph to this chapter highlights the rather different constitutional position that puts Canadian negotiators under increasing pressure from their major trading partners.

Where Do We Go From Here?

The context of this study is a general interest in the responses of states to market forces, especially whether or not this adaptation is likely to lead to political-institutional convergence, both at the domestic and macro-regional levels (Boyer, 1996; Drezner, 2001; Hülsemeyer, 2003). While this thesis focused on the member states of what are considered 'successful' integration schemes (Mattli, 1999), there are two directions of further research that would seem to follow from the findings presented here.

First, a comparison of the EU and NAFTA with other regional integration schemes, particularly Mercosur and ASEAN, could establish the extent to which these four macro-regions react in their developments to each other, if so, potentially setting in motion a 'spiral' of regional integration. In other words, the question is whether or not any 'logic of regional integration' (Mattli, 1999) indeed exists.

Second, apart from the supranationalization of public sector functions, the second political-institutional trend in the adaptation to economic globalization is the devolution of competencies to different subnational levels of government. This process can be observed to varying degrees in federal and unitary states alike. Similar to the shifting of powers upward, the question of constitutional convergence arises. This includes investigating the extent to which it continues to make a difference whether countries are federally or unitarily constituted.

The question of convergence was also at the heart of the epigraph that provided the starting point for this book. The investigation gives credence to the assertion implicit in Laski's more than 60-year-old assessment that a more centralized form of government is more conducive to responding to international economic pressures than a decentralized federation with a larger number of institutional veto players. In practical terms, the findings of this analysis might travel beyond strictly federally constituted countries. The distinction between centralized and decentralized political systems appears to have implications for the concrete form of the decentralization projects underway in unitary states, among others, the United Kingdom and France.

Federalism is *not* 'alive and well' in all countries which have formally adopted it; its rationale *may* still be put forward to accommodate the cultural and/or ethnic differences within a society but the *economic* advantages over unitary states are rather unconvincing.[8] With the findings on the German federation in mind, the epoch of federalism certainly is not over *de jure*, but it may *de facto* be a step closer to its obsolescence.

Notes

1 In other words, I do *not* disagree with the conception of institutional veto players as outlined by him. Rather I hold that its application in the strict form in which he formulates it is not as easily transferable to an examination of the domestic adjustment process to internationalization as Garrett and Lange (1996) imply.

2 The provincial participation during the CUSFTA received enormous scholarly coverage, as this was the first time a formal process of consultations had been established. The CUSFTA was *expected* to touch on matters under provincial jurisdiction in a wide range of areas.

Academic and public attention to the provincial role was virtually absent during the NAFTA negotiations; the trilateral agreement was largely viewed as an extension of the CUSFTA to Mexico that did not warrant special attention to provincial interests, although the NAFTA side agreements fell squarely into provincial jurisdiction. The participation of the component governments during the multilateral trade negotiations of the Uruguay Round under the auspices of the GATT shared the same fate of academic disinterest (see below).

3 To be sure, Fiscal Federalism does not question the mediating role of extant institutions in principle. Instead, it articulates which level of government is welfare optimal for the provision of a particular public sector function under conditions of globalization. It proposes what government change should *ideally* look like, *regardless* of societal preferences and extant institutions. This contrasts with the null hypothesis, which *denies* that domestic institutions have any influence at all.

4 While most macro-regions, particularly NAFTA, are considered reactions to accelerated European integration since the mid-1980s (Mayer, 1998; Mattli, 1999), NAFTA is unlikely to converge on the European 'model' (Whalley, 1992).

5 Note that the differences in opinion over agriculture are not merely a 'simple' trade topic; instead, they also reflect fundamentally different perspectives on the *role* of this sector. For the United States, agriculture is in principle like production in any other sector of an economy, whereas the EU sees it in much broader terms, reflecting environmental concerns (caretaking of the land) and being a cornerstone of the social fabric of society. The EU is now justifying its agricultural subsidies on this basis, while the United States sees this as a mere excuse for protectionist trade practices.

6 Correspondence with Helmut Mach, Executive Director for Trade Policy, Government of Alberta, on 20 November 2001; Mr. Mach headed the provincial delegation in Geneva.

7 Canada was proposing 'tariff equivalents of 283.8 per cent for milk, 351.4 per cent for butter, 289 per cent for cheddar cheese, 280.4 per cent for chicken and 192.3 per cent for eggs' (Chapman, 1996: 18).

8 Riker (1964) charged that even the defence of federalism on cultural and ethnic grounds had disastrous effects in the United States where he claims it allowed slavery and racial segregation in the southern states to be maintained for as long as it did. Cairns (1995) uses the example of the large number of visible minorities in Toronto and Vancouver to suggest that federalism as a *territorial* principle is unsuitable in such an environment nowadays, as the cultural and ethnic divisions are evident more in large cities rather than being geographically concentrated. Instead, echoing Riker, Cairns points to the risk of creating 'minorities within minorities' in a federal order.

Bibliography

Abelson, Donald E. and Lusztig, Michael (1996), 'The consistency of inconsistency: tracing Ontario's opposition to the North American Free Trade Agreement', *Canadian Journal of Political Science*, 29 (4): 681–98.

Anonymous (1988), 'Issues of Constitutional Jurisdiction', in Peter M. Leslie and Ronald L. Watts (eds), *Canada: The State of the Federation 1987–88*, Kingston, ON: Institute of Intergovernmental Relations, Queen's University, pp. 39–55.

Archer, Margaret S. (1996), *Culture and Agency: The Place of Culture in Social Theory*, 2nd rev. edn, Cambridge: Cambridge University Press.

Avery, William P. and Friman, Richard H. (1999), 'Who Got What and Why: Constructing North American Free Trade', in Kenneth P. Thomas and Mary Ann Tetréault (eds), *Racing to Regionalize: Democracy, Capitalism, and Regional Political Economy*, Boulder, CO: Lynne Rienner, pp. 87–112.

Bakvis, Herman and Chandler, William M. (1987a), 'Federalism in Comparative Analysis', in Herman Bakvis and William M. Chandler (eds), *Federalism and the Role of the State*, Toronto: University of Toronto Press, pp. 3–11.

Bakvis, Herman and Chandler, William M. (1987b), 'The Future of Federalism', in Herman Bakvis and William M. Chandler (eds), *Federalism and the Role of the State*, Toronto: University of Toronto Press, pp. 306–18.

Benz, Arthur (2000), 'Two types of multi-level governance: intergovernmental relations in German and EU regional policy', *Regional & Federal Studies*, 10 (3): 21–44.

Bernstein, Steven and Cashore, Benjamin (2000), 'Globalization, four paths of internationalization and domestic policy change: the case of ecoforestry in British Columbia, Canada', *Canadian Journal of Political Science*, 33 (1): 67–99.

Beukel, Erik (1999), 'Trade Liberalization and Environmental Regulations: Regional Interests and Ideas in Europe and North America', in Kenneth P. Thomas and Mary Ann Tetréault (eds), *Racing to Regionalize: Democracy, Capitalism, and Regional Political Economy*, Boulder, CO: Lynne Rienner, pp. 113–39.

Blair, Philip and Cullen, Peter (1999), 'Federalism, Legalism and Political Reality: The Record of the Federal Constitutional Court', in Charlie Jeffery (ed.), *Recasting German Federalism: The Legacies of Unification*, London: Pinter, pp. 119–54.

Boadway, Robin (2000), 'Recent Developments in the Economics of

Federalism', in Harvey Lazaar (ed.), *Toward a New Mission Statement for Canadian Fiscal Federalism* (Canada: The State of the Federation 1999/2000), Kingston, ON: McGill-Queen's University Press, pp. 41–78.

Boadway, Robin and Keen, Michael (1997), 'Efficiency and the Optimal Direction of Federal-State Transfers', in David E. Wildasin (ed.), *Fiscal Aspects of Evolving Federations*, New York: Cambridge University Press, pp. 41–62.

Boeckelman, Keith (1996), 'Federal systems in the global economy: research issues', *Publius: the Journal of Federalism*, 26 (1): 1–10.

Bornschier, Volker (ed.) (2000), *State-building in Europe: The Revitalization of Western European Integration*, Cambridge: Cambridge University Press.

Bowles, Paul and MacLean, Brian (1996), 'Understanding trade bloc formation: the case of the ASEAN free trade area', *Review of International Political Economy*, 3 (2): 319–48.

Boyer, Robert (1996), 'The Convergence Hypothesis Revisited: Globalization But Still the Century of Nations?, in Suzanne Berger and Ronald Dore (eds), *National Diversity and Global Capitalism*, Ithaca, NY: Cornell University Press, pp. 29–59.

Brenner, Neil (1998), 'Global cities, glocal states: global city formation and state territorial restructuring in contemporary Europe', *Review of International Political Economy*, 5 (1): 1–37.

Brown, Douglas M. (1988), 'The Federal-Provincial Consultation Process', in Peter M. Leslie and Ronald L. Watts (eds), *Canada: The State of the Federation 1987–88*, Kingston, ON: Institute of Intergovernmental Relations, Queen's University, pp. 77–93.

——— (1989), 'Canadian Federalism and Trade Policy: The Uruguay Round Agenda', in Ronald L. Watts and Douglas M. Brown (eds), *Canada: The State of the Federation 1989*, Kingston, ON: Institute of Intergovernmental Relations, Queen's University, pp. 211–35.

Brown, Douglas M. and Smith, Murray C. (eds) (1991), *Canadian Federalism: Meeting Global Economic Challenges?*, Kingston, ON: Institute of Intergovernmental Relations, Queen's University.

Burgess, Michael and Gress, Franz (1993), 'The Quest for a Federal Future: German Unity and European Union', in Michael Burgess and Alain-G. Gagnon (eds), *Comparative Federalism and Federation: Competing Traditions and Future Directions*, Toronto: University of Toronto Press, pp. 168–86.

Burley, Anne-Marie and Mattli, Walter (1993), 'Europe before the court: a political theory of legal integration', *International Organization*, 47 (1): 41–76.

Cairns, Alan C. (1995), 'Constitutional Government and the Two Faces of Ethnicity: Federalism is Not Enough', in Karen Knop, Sylvia Ostry, Richard Simeon and Katherine Swinton (eds), *Rethinking Federalism: Citizens, Markets, and Governments in a Changing World*, Vancouver: University of British Columbia Press, pp. 15–39.

Calvert, John (1988), 'Government Procurement', in Duncan Cameron (ed.), *The Free Trade Deal*, Toronto: James Lorimer & Company, pp. 131–9.

Cameron, Maxwell A. and Tomlin, Brian W. (2000), *The Making of NAFTA: How the Deal Was Done*, Ithaca, NY: Cornell University Press.

Carlsnaes, Walter (1992), 'The agency-structure problem in foreign policy analysis', *International Studies Quarterly*, 36: 245–70.

Cerny, Philip G. (1991), 'The limits of deregulation: transnational interpenetration and policy change', *European Journal of Political Research*, 19: 173–96.

——— (1995), 'Globalization and the changing logic of collective action', *International Organization*, 49 (4): 595–625.

——— (1996), 'Globalization and other stories: the search for a new paradigm for International Relations', *International Journal*, 51: 617–37.

——— (1997), 'Paradoxes of the competition state: the dynamics of political globalization', *Government and Opposition*, 32 (2): 251–74.

——— (1999), 'Globalization, Governance, and Complexity', in Aseem Prakash and Jeffrey A. Hart (eds), *Globalization and Governance*, London: Routledge, pp. 188–212.

Chapman, Anthony (1996), *Multilateral Trade Negotiations* (Paper 87–14E), Ottawa: Research Branch, Library of Parliament.

Clayton, Richard and Pontusson, Jonas (1998), 'Welfare-state retrenchment revisited: entitlement cuts, public sector restructuring, and inegalitarian trends in advanced capitalist societies', *World Politics*, 51 (1): 67–98.

Cohen, Benjamin J. (1998), *The Geography of Money*, Ithaca, NY: Cornell University Press.

Coleman, William D. and Underhill, Geoffrey R.D. (eds) (1998), *Regionalism and Global Economic Integration: Europe, Asia and the Americas*, London: Routledge.

Courchene, Thomas J. (1996), 'Preserving and Promoting the Internal Economic Union: Australia and Canada', in Paul Boothe (ed.), *Reforming Fiscal Federalism for Global Competition: A Canada-Australia Comparison*, Edmonton: The University of Alberta Press, pp. 185–222.

Cowles, Maria G. (1995), 'Setting the agenda for a new Europe: the ERT and EC 1992', *Journal of Common Market Studies*, 33 (4): 501–26.

Cremer, Helmuth, Marchand, Maurice and Pestieau, Pierre (1997), 'Interregional Redistribution through Tax Surcharge', in David E. Wildasin (ed.), *Fiscal Aspects of Evolving Federations*, New York: Cambridge University Press, pp. 63–81.

Crouch, Colin and Streeck, Wolfgang (eds) (1997), *Political Economy of Capitalism: Mapping Convergence and Diversity*, London: Sage.

Deeg, Richard (1996), 'Economic globalization and the shifting boundaries of German federalism', *Publius: the Journal of Federalism*, 26 (1): 27–52.

Deeg, Richard and Lütz, Susanne (2000), 'Internationalization and financial federalism: the United States and Germany at the crossroads?', *Comparative Political Studies*, 33 (3): 374–405.

Dehousse, Renaud (1992), 'Integration v. regulation?: on the dynamics of regulation in the European Community', *Journal of Common Market Studies*, 30 (4): 383–402.

Delagran, Leslie (1992), 'Conflict in trade policy: the role of the congress and the provinces in negotiating and implementing the Canada-U.S. free trade agreement', *Publius: the Journal of Federalism*, 22 (4): 15–29.

Dessler, David (1989), 'What's at stake in the agent-structure debate?', *International Organization*, 43 (3): 441–73.

Doern, Bruce G. and Tomlin, Brian W. (1991), *Faith and Fear: The Free Trade Story*, Toronto: Stoddart.

Drezner, Daniel W. (2001), 'Globalization and policy convergence', *International Studies Review*, 3 (1): 53–78.

Duchacek, Ivo D. (1970), *Comparative Federalism: The Territorial Dimension of Politics*, New York: Holt, Rinehart and Winston.

Dunn, Sheilagh M. (1988), 'The Free Trade Initiative and Regional Strategies', in Peter M. Leslie and Ronald L. Watts (eds), *Canada: The State of the Federation 1987–88*, Kingston, ON: Institute of Intergovernmental Relations, Queen's University, pp. 57–76.

Dupras, Daniel (1993), *NAFTA: Implementation and the Participation of the Provinces* (Background Paper BP–324E), Ottawa: Research Branch, Library of Parliament.

Eckstein, Harry (1975), 'Case Study and Theory in Political Science', in Fred I. Greenstein and Nelson, W. Polsby (eds), *Handbook of Political Science, vol. 7, Strategies of Inquiry*, Reading, MA: Addison-Wesley, pp. 79–137.

Esping-Andersen, Gøsta (1990), *The Three Worlds of Welfare Capitalism*, Cambridge: Polity Press.

Evans, Peter (1997), 'The eclipse of the state?: reflections on stateness in an era of globalization', *World Politics*, 50 (1): 62–87.

Fairley, H. Scott (1986), 'Constitutional Aspects of External Trade Policy', in Mark Krasnick (ed.), *Case Studies in the Division of Powers*, Toronto: University of Toronto Press, pp. 1–51.

Falk, Richard (1997), 'State of siege: will globalization win out?', *International Affairs*, 73 (1): 123–36.

Feigenbaum, Harvey, Henig, Jeffrey and Hamnett, Chris (1998), *Shrinking the State: The Political Underpinnings of Privatization*, Cambridge: Cambridge University Press.

Fiedler, Nicola (2000), 'The Origins of the Single Market', in Volker Bornschier (ed.), *State-building in Europe: The Revitalization of Western European Integration*, Cambridge: Cambridge University Press, pp. 75–92.

Fitzgerald, Niall (1997), 'Harnessing the potential of globalization for the consumer and citizen', *International Affairs*, 73 (4): 739–46.

Frey, Bruno S. (1978), *Modern Political Economy*, New York: John Wiley & Sons.

Frieden, Jeffry A. (1991), 'Invested interests: the politics of national economic policies in a world of global finance', *International Organization*, 45 (4): 425–51.

——— (1997), 'Economic Liberalization and the Politics of European Monetary Integration', in Miles Kahler (ed.), *Liberalization and Foreign Policy*, New York: Columbia University Press, pp. 237–68.

Frieden, Jeffry A. and Rogowski, Ronald (1996), 'The Impact of the International Economy on National Policies: An Analytical Overview', in Robert O. Keohane and Helen V. Milner (eds), *Internationalization and Domestic Politics*, New York: Cambridge University Press, pp. 25–47.

Friedrich, Carl J. (1969), *Europe: An Emergent Nation?*, New York: Harper & Row.

Garman, Christopher, Haggard, Stephan and Willis, Eliza (2001), 'Fiscal decentralization: a political theory with Latin American cases', *World Politics*, 53 (2): 205–36.

Garrett, Geoffrey (1992), 'International cooperation and institutional choice: the European Community's internal market', *International Organization*, 46 (2): 533–60.

——— (1998a), *Partisan Politics in the Global Economy*, New York: Cambridge University Press.

——— (1998b), 'Global markets and national politics: collision course or virtuous circle?', *International Organization*, 52 (4): 787–824.

Garrett, Geoffrey and Lange, Peter (1996), 'Internationalization, Institutions, and Political Change', in Robert O. Keohane and Helen V. Milner (eds), *Internationalization and Domestic Politics*, New York: Cambridge University Press, pp. 48–75.

Gibbins, Roger (1987), 'Federal Societies, Institutions, and Politics', in Herman Bakvis and William M. Chandler (eds), *Federalism and the Role of the State*, Toronto: University of Toronto Press, pp. 15–31.

Goetz, Klaus H. (1995), 'National governance and European integration: intergovernmental relations in Germany', *Journal of Common Market Studies*, 33 (1): 91–116.

Gress, Franz (1996), 'Interstate cooperation and territorial representation in intermestic politics', *Publius: the Journal of Federalism*, 26 (1): 53–71.

Gunlicks, Arthur B. (1994), 'German federalism after unification: the legal/constitutional response', *Publius: the Journal of Federalism*, 24 (2): 81–98.

Haas, Ernst B. (1958), *The Uniting of Europe: Political, Social, and Economical Forces, 1950–1957*, Stanford: Stanford University Press.

Hanson, Brian T. (1998), 'What happened to fortress Europe?: external trade policy liberalization in the European Union', *International Organization*, 52 (1): 55–85.

Hart, Michael (1998), *Fifty Years of Canadian Tradecraft: Canada at the GATT 1947–1997*, Ottawa: Centre for Trade Policy and Law, Carleton University.

Haverland, Markus (2000), 'National adaptation to European integration: the importance of institutional veto points', *Journal of Public Policy*, 20 (1): 83–103.

Helleiner, Eric (1997), 'Braudelian Reflections on Economic Globalisation: The Historian as Pioneer', in Stephen Gill and James A. Mittelman (eds), *Innovation and Transformation in International Studies*, Cambridge: Cambridge University Press, pp. 90–104.

Hirsch, Joachim (1997), 'Globalization of capital, nation-states, and democracy', *Studies in Political Economy*, 54: 39–58.

Hirst, Paul and Thompson, Graham (1995), 'Globalization and the future of the nation state', *Economy and Society*, 24 (3): 408–42.

Hobson, John M. (2000), *The State and International Relations*, Cambridge: Cambridge University Press.

Hooghe, Liesbet (1995), 'Subnational mobilisation in the European Union', *West European Politics*, 18 (3): 175–98.

Hrbek, Rudolf (1999), 'The Effects of EU Integration on German Federalism', in Charlie Jeffery (ed.), *Recasting German Federalism: The Legacies of Unification*, London: Pinter, pp. 217–33.

Hueglin, Thomas O. (1990), *A Political Economy of Federalism: In Search of a New Comparative Perspective with Critical Intent Throughout*, Kingston, ON: Institute of Intergovernmental Relations, Queen's University.

Hülsemeyer, Axel (2000), 'Changing "political economies of scale" and public sector adjustment: insights from fiscal federalism', *Review of International Political Economy*, 7 (1): 72–100.

——— (ed.) (2003), *Globalization in the Twenty-First Century: Convergence or Divergence*?, London: Palgrave Macmillan.

——— (forthcoming), *Toward Deeper North American Integration?* (Canadian-American Public Policy Occasional Paper), Orono, ME: Canadian-American Center, University of Maine.

Jaquet, Pierre (1998), 'EMU: a worthwile gamble', *International Affairs*, 74 (1): 55–72.

Jeffery, Charlie (1996), 'Towards a "third level" in Europe?: the German Länder in the European Union', *Political Studies*, 44: 253–66.

Jenkins, Barbara (1999), 'Assessing the "New" Integration: The Mercosur Trade Agreement', in Kenneth P. Thomas and Mary Ann Tetréault (eds), *Racing to Regionalize: Democracy, Capitalism, and Regional Political Economy*, Boulder, CO: Lynne Rienner, pp. 33–56.

Johnson, Nevil (1999), 'Territory and Power: Some Historical Determinants of the Constitutional Structure of the Federal Republic of Germany', in Charlie Jeffery (ed.), *Recasting German Federalism: The Legacies of Unification*, London: Pinter, pp. 23–39.

Jones, Robert A. (1996), *The Politics and Economics of the European Union: An Introductory Text*, Cheltenham: Edward Elgar.

Julius, Deanne (1997), 'Globalization and stakeholder conflicts: a corporate perspective', *International Affairs*, 73 (3): 453–68.

Kelemen, R. Daniel (2000), 'Regulatory federalism: EU environmental regulation in comparative perspective', *Journal of Public Policy*, 20 (2): 133–67.

Keohane, Robert O. and Hoffmann, Stanley (1991), 'Institutional Change in Europe in the 1980s', in Robert O. Keohane and Stanley Hoffmann (eds), *The New European Community: Decisionmaking and Institutional Change*, Boulder, CO: Westview Press, pp. 1–39.

Keohane, Robert O. and Milner, Helen V. (eds) (1996), *Internationalization and Domestic Politics*, New York: Cambridge University Press.

King, Gary, Keohane, Robert O. and Verba, Sidney (1994), *Designing Social Inquiry: Scientific Inference in Qualitative Research*, Princeton, NJ: Princeton University Press.

Klatt, Hartmut (1999), 'Centralizing Trends in West German Federalism, 1949–89', in Charlie Jeffery (ed.), *Recasting German Federalism: The Legacies of Unification*, London: Pinter, pp. 40–57.

Lane, Jan-Erik (1995), *The Public Sector: Concepts, Models and Approaches*, 2nd rev. edn, London: Sage.

Laski, Harold (1939), 'The obsolescence of federalism', *The New Republic: A Journal of Opinion*, 3 May: 367–9.

Lawson, Fred H. (1999), 'Theories of Integration in a New Context: The Gulf Cooperation Council', in Kenneth P. Thomas and Mary Ann Tetréault (eds), *Racing to Regionalize: Democracy, Capitalism, and Regional Political Economy*, Boulder, CO: Lynne Rienner, pp. 7–31.

Lazar, Harvey, Telford, Hamish and Watts, Ronald L. (eds) (2003), *The Impact of Global and Regional Integration on Federal Systems: A Comparative Analysis*, Montreal: McGill Queen's University Press.

Lazonick, William (1991), *Business Organization and the Myth of the Market Economy*, New York: Cambridge University Press.

Leonardy, Uwe (1999a), 'The Institutional Structures of German Federalism', in Charlie Jeffery (ed.), *Recasting German Federalism: The Legacies of Unification*, London: Pinter, pp. 3–22.

——— (1999b), 'German Federalism Towards 2000: To Be Reformed or Deformed?', in Charlie Jeffery (ed.), *Recasting German Federalism: The Legacies of Unification*, London: Pinter, pp. 285–311.

Lowi, Theodore (1964), 'American business, public policy, case studies, and political theory', *World Politics*, 16 (4): 677–715.

Lipsey, Richard G., Schwanen, Daniel and Wonnacott, Ronald J. (1994), *The NAFTA: What's In, What's Out, What's Next*, Toronto: C.D. Howe Institute.

Lusztig, Michael and James, Patrick (1996), 'Constitutional reform and the free trade agreement in Canada: political entrepreneurship and the quest for realignment', *International Journal of Canadian Studies*, 14: 239–55.

Majone, Giandomenico (1993), 'The European Community between social policy and social regulation', *Journal of Common Market Studies*, 31 (2): 153–70.

Malcomson, Patrick and Myers, Richard (1996), *The Canadian Regime*, Scarborough, ON: Broadview Press.

Mansfield, Edward D. and Milner, Helen V. (1999), 'The new wave of regionalism', *International Organization*, 53 (3): 589–627.

Marks, Gary, Nielsen, François, Ray, Leonhard and Salk, Jane E. (1996), 'Competencies, cracks, and conflicts: regional mobilization in the European Union', *Comparative Political Studies*, 29 (2): 164–92.

Mattli, Walter (1999), *The Logic of Regional Integration: Europe and Beyond*, Cambridge: Cambridge University Press.

Mayer, Frederick W. (1998), *Interpreting NAFTA: The Science and Art of Political Analysis*, New York: Columbia University Press.

McIlroy, James P. (1997), 'NAFTA and the Canadian provinces: two ships passing in the night?', *Canada-United States Law Journal*, 23: 431–40.

McKinney, Joseph A. (2000), *Created from NAFTA: The Structure, Function, and Significance of the Treaty's Related Institutions*, Armonk, NY: M. E. Sharpe.

McKinnon, Ronald I. (1963), 'Optimum currency areas', *American Economic Review*, 53: 717–24.

McWhinney, Edward (1962), *Comparative Federalism*, Toronto: University of Toronto Press.

Michelmann, Hans J. (1986), 'Federalism and international relations in Canada and the Federal Republic of Germany', *International Journal*, 41 (3): 539–71.

Milner, Helen V. and Keohane, Robert O. (1996), 'Internationalization and Domestic Politics: An Introduction', in Robert O. Keohane and Helen V. Milner (eds), *Internationalization and Domestic Politics*, New York: Cambridge University Press, pp. 3–24.

Miner, William M. (1993), *From NAFTA to GATT and Back to NAFTA* (Occasional Papers in International Trade Law and Policy, No. 34), Ottawa: Centre for Trade Policy and Law, Carleton University.

Money, Jeannette and Tsebelis, George (1992), 'Cicero's puzzle: upper house power in comparative perspective', *International Political Science Review*, 13 (1): 25–43.

Moravcsik, Andrew (1991), 'Negotiating the Single European Act: national interest and conventional statecraft in the European Community', *International Organization*, 45 (1): 19–56.

Mueller, Dennis C. (1979), Public Choice, New York: Cambridge University Press.

Müller-Brandeck-Bocquet, Gisela (1992), 'Europäische Integration und deutscher Föderalismus', in Michael Kreile (ed.), *Die Integration Europas* (PVS Sonderheft 23/1992), Opladen: Westdeutscher Verlag, pp. 160–82.

Nass, Klaus Otto (1989), 'The foreign and European policy of the German Länder', *Publius: the Journal of Federalism*, 19 (4): 165–84.

Norrie, Kenneth (1995), 'Is Federalism the Future?: An Economic Perspective', in Karen Knop, Sylvia Ostry, Richard Simeon and Katherine Swinton (eds), *Rethinking Federalism: Citizens, Markets, and Governments in a Changing World*, Vancouver: University of British Columbia Press, pp. 135–53.

Oates, Wallace E. (1972), *Fiscal Federalism*, New York: Harcourt Brace Jovanovich.

——— (1977), 'An Economist's Perspective on Fiscal Federalism', in Wallace E. Oates (ed.), *The Political Economy of Fiscal Federalism*, Lexington, MA: Lexington Books, pp. 3–20.

——— (1991), *Studies in Fiscal Federalism*, Aldershot, UK: Edward Elgar.

——— (1999), 'An essay on fiscal federalism', *Journal of Economic Literature*, 37 (3): 1120–49.

O'Brien, Robert (1995), 'North American integration and international relations theory', *Canadian Journal of Political Science*, 28 (4): 693–724.

Ohmae, Kenichi (1995), *The End of the Nation State: The Rise of Regional Economies*, New York: Free Press.

Olson, Mancur (1965), *The Logic of Collective Action: Public Goods and the Theory of Groups*, Cambridge, MA: Harvard University Press.

Ostrom, Vincent, Tiebout, Charles M. and Warren, Robert (1961), 'The organization of government in metropolitan areas: a theoretical inquiry', *American Political Science Review*, 55 (4): 831–42.

Ostrom, Vincent and Ostrom, Elinor (1977), 'Public Goods and Public Choices', in Emanuel S. Savas (ed.), *Alternatives for Delivering Public Services: Toward Improved Performance*, Boulder, CO: Westview Press, pp. 7–49.

Paarlberg, Robert (1997), 'Agricultural policy reform and the Uruguay Round: synergistic linkage in a two-level game?', *International Organization*, 51 (3): 413–44.

Padoa-Schioppa, Tommaso (1995), 'Economic Federalism and the European Union', in Karen Knop, Sylvia Ostry, Richard Simeon and Katherine Swinton (eds), *Rethinking Federalism: Citizens, Markets, and Governments in a Changing World*, Vancouver: University of British Columbia Press, pp. 154–65.

Painter, Martin (1991), 'Intergovernmental relations in Canada: an institutional analysis', *Canadian Journal of Political Science*, 24 (2): 269–88.

Parker, Simon (2000), 'Esprit and Technology Corporatism', in Volker Bornschier (ed.), *State-building in Europe: The Revitalization of Western European Integration*, Cambridge: Cambridge University Press, pp. 93–121.

Pauly, Louis W. and Reich, Simon (1997), 'National structures and multinational corporate behavior: enduring differences in the age of globalization', *International Organization*, 51 (1): 1–30.

Pérez, Sofia A. (2000), 'From decentralization to reorganization: explaining the return to national bargaining in Italy and Spain', *Comparative Politics*, 32 (4): 437–58.

Pierson, Paul (1996a), 'The new politics of the welfare state', *World Politics*, 48 (2): 143–79.

——— (1996b), 'The path to European integration: a historical institutionalist analysis', *Comparative Political Studies*, 29 (2): 123–63.

——— (2000a), 'Increasing returns, path dependence, and the study of politics', *American Political Science Review*, 94 (2): 251–67.
——— (2000b), 'The limits of design: explaining institutional origins and change', *Governance: an International Journal of Policy and Administration*, 13 (4): 475–99.
Pinder, John (1996), 'Economic and Monetary Union: pillar of a federal polity', *Publius: the Journal of Federalism*, 26 (4): 123–40.
Prakash, Aseem and Hart, Jeffrey A. (eds) (1999), *Globalization and Governance*, London: Routledge.
——— (2000), 'Indicators of economic integration', *Global Governance*, 6: 95–114.
Regini, Marino (2000), 'Between deregulation and social pacts: the responses of European economies to globalization', *Politics & Society*, 28 (1): 5–33.
Reich, Simon (2000), 'The four phases of institutionalism: public policy and a pluralistic perspective', *Governance: An International Journal of Policy and Administration*, 13 (4): 501–22.
Reischauer, Robert D. (1977), 'Governmental Diversity: Bane of the Grants Strategy in the United States', in Wallace E. Oates (ed.), *The Political Economy of Fiscal Federalism*, Lexington, MA: Lexington Books, pp. 115–27.
Rhodes, Martin (1992), 'The future of the "social dimension": labour market regulation in post-1992 Europe', *Journal of Common Market Studies*, 30 (1): 23–51.
——— (1998), ' "Subversive Liberalism": Market Integration, Globalization and West European Welfare States', in William D. Coleman and Geoffrey R. D. Underhill (eds), *Regionalism and Global Economic Integration: Europe, Asia and the Americas*, London: Routledge, pp. 99–121.
Richards, Robert G. (1991), 'The Canadian Constitution and International Economic Relations', in Douglas M. Brown and Murray G. Smith (eds), *Canadian Federalism: Meeting Global Economic Challenges?*, Kingston, ON: Institute of Intergovernmental Relations, Queen's University, pp. 57–63.
Riker, William H. (1964), *Federalism: Origin, Operation, Significance*, Boston: Little, Brown.
Ritchie, Gordon (1997), *Wrestling with the Elephant: The Inside Story of the Canada-US Trade Wars*, Toronto: Macfarlane Walter & Ross.
Robinson, Ian (1993), 'The NAFTA, the Side-Deals, and Canadian Federalism: Constitutional Reform by Other Means?', in Ronald L. Watts and Douglas M. Brown (eds), *Canada: The State of the Federation 1993*, Kingston, ON: Institute of Intergovernmental Relations, Queen's University, pp. 193–227.
Rockman, Bert A. (1994), 'The New Institutionalism and the Old Institutions', in Lawrence C. Dodd and Calvin Jillson (eds), *New Perspectives on American Politics*, Washington, DC: CQ Press, pp. 143–61.

Rosenau, James N. (1997), *Along the Domestic-Foreign Frontier: Exploring Governance in a Turbulent World*, Cambridge: Cambridge University Press.

Ruggie, John G. (1998), *Constructing the World Polity: Essays on International Institutionalization*, London: Routledge.

Rugman, Alan M. (1994), 'North American Economic Integration and Canadian Sovereignty', in M. Delal Baer and Sidney Weintraub (eds), *The NAFTA Debate: Grappling with Unconventional Trade Issues*, Boulder, CO: Lynne Rienner, pp. 97–116.

Rupert, Mark E. (1995), '(Re)Politicizing the global economy: liberal common sense and ideological struggle in the US NAFTA debate', *Review of International Political Economy*, 2 (4): 658–92.

Sandholtz, Wayne (1993), 'Choosing union: monetary politics and Maastricht', *International Organization*, 37 (1): 1–39.

Sandholtz, Wayne and Zysman, John (1989), '1992: recasting the European bargain', *World Politics*, 42 (1): 95–128.

Saunders, Cheryl (1995), 'Constitutional arrangements of federal systems', *Publius: The Journal of Federalism*, 25 (2): 61–79.

Schaefer, Matthew (1997,) 'Searching for Pareto gains in the relationship between free trade and federalism: revisiting the NAFTA, eyeing the FTAA', *Canada-United States Law Journal*, 23: 441–94.

Scharpf, Fritz W. (1994), *Chancen des Föderalismus in Deutschland und Europa*, Frankfurt a. M.: Campus.

——— (2000), 'Institutions in comparative policy research', *Comparative Political Studies*, 33 (6/7): 762–90.

Schmidt, Vivien A. (1999), 'European "federalism" and its encroachments on national institutions', *Publius: The Journal of Federalism*, 29 (1): 19–44.

Schneider, Hans-Peter (1999), 'German Unification and the Federal System: The Challenge of Reform', in Charlie Jeffery (ed.), *Recasting German Federalism: The Legacies of Unification*, London: Pinter, pp. 58–84.

Shoch, James (2000), 'Contesting globalization: organized labor, NAFTA, and the 1997 and 1998 fast-track fights', *Politics & Society*, 28 (1): 119–50.

Siaroff, Alan (1999), 'Corporatism in 24 industrial democracies: meaning and measurement', *European Journal of Political Research*, 36 (2): 175–205.

Simeon, Richard (1986), 'Federalism and Free Trade', in Peter M. Leslie (ed.), *Canada: The State of the Federation 1986*, Kingston, ON: Institute of Intergovernmental Relations, Queen's University, pp. 189–212.

Snyder, Richard (1999), 'After neoliberalism: the politics of reregulation in Mexico', *World Politics*, 51: 173–204.

Springer, Beverly (1992), *The Social Dimension of 1992: Europe Faces a New EC*, Westport, CT: Greenwood Press.

Spruyt, Hendrik (1994), *The Sovereign State and Its Competitors: An Analysis of Systems Change*, Princeton, NJ: Princeton University Press.

Strange, Susan (1994), *States and Markets*, 2nd edn, London: Pinter.

——— (1996), *The Retreat of the State: The Diffusion of Power in the World Economy*, Cambridge: Cambridge University Press.

Streeck, Wolfgang and Schmitter, Philippe C. (1991), 'From national corporatism to transnational pluralism: organized interests in the Single European Market', *Politics & Society*, 19 (2): 133–64.

Stubbs, Richard (1998), 'Asia-Pacific Regionalism Versus Globalization: Competing Forms of Capitalism', in William D. Coleman and Geoffrey R.D. Underhill (eds), *Regionalism and Global Economic Integration: Europe, Asia and the Americas*, London: Routledge, pp. 68–80.

Sun, Jeanne-Mey and Pelkmans, Jacques (1995), 'Regulatory competition in the Single Market', *Journal of Common Market Studies*, 33 (1): 67–89.

Thelen, Kathleen and Kume, Ikuo (1999), 'The effects of globalization revisited: lessons from Germany and Japan', *Politics & Society*, 27 (4): 477–505.

Thorlakson, Lori (2000), 'Government building and political development in federations: applying Canadian theory to the German case', *Regional & Federal Studies*, 10 (3): 129–48.

Tiebout, Charles M. (1956), 'A pure theory of local expenditure', *Journal of Political Economy*, 44: 416–24.

Tsebelis, George (1995), 'Decision making in political systems: veto players in presidentialism, parliamentarism, multicameralism and multipartyism', *British Journal of Political Science*, 25: 289–325.

——— (2000), 'Veto players and institutional analysis', *Governance: an International Journal of Policy and Administration*, 13 (4): 441–74.

Underhill, Geoffrey R. D. (2000), 'Introduction: Conceptualizing the Changing Global Order', in Richard Stubbs and Geoffrey R. D. Underhill (eds), *Political Economy and the Changing Global Order*, 2nd edn, Don Mills, ON: Oxford University Press, pp. 3–24.

Van Evera, Stephen (1997) *Guide to Methods for Students of Political Science*, Ithaca, NY: Cornell University Press.

Waltz, Kenneth N. (1979), *Theory of International Politics*, New York: McGraw-Hill.

Walz, Uwe and Wellisch, Dietmar (1997), 'Strategic Provision of Local Public Inputs for Oligopolistic Firms in the Presence of Endogenous Location Choice', in David E. Wildasin (ed.), *Fiscal Aspects of Evolving Federations*, New York: Cambridge University Press, pp. 120–38.

Watts, Ronald L. (1999), 'German Federalism in Comparative Perspective', in Charlie Jeffery (ed.) *Recasting German Federalism: The Legacies of Unification*, London: Pinter, pp. 265–84.

Wehling, Hans-Georg (1989), 'The Bundesrat', *Publius: the Journal of Federalism*, 19 (4): 53–64.

Weiler, J.H.H. (2000), 'Epilogue: Towards a Common Law of International Trade', in J.H.H. Weiler (ed.), *The EU, the WTO, and the NAFTA*, New York: Oxford University Press, pp. 201–32.

Weiler, Todd (1999), *Identifying, Implementing, and Enforcing International*

Regulatory Reform Obligations: The Canadian Experience (Occasional Papers in International Trade Law and Policy, No. 53), Ottawa: Centre for Trade Policy and Law, Carleton University.

Wendt, Alexander (1987), 'The agent-structure problem in international relations theory', *International Organization*, 41 (3): 335–70.

——— (1992) 'Levels of analysis vs. agents and structures: part III', *Review of International Studies*, 18: 181–5.

Whalley, John (1992), 'CUSTA and NAFTA: can WHFTA be far behind?', *Journal of Common Market Studies*, 30 (2): 125–41.

Wheare, K.C. (1953), *Federal Government*, 3rd edn, Oxford: Oxford University Press.

Whittington, Michael S. and Van Loon, Richard J. (1996), *Canadian Government and Politics: Institutions and Processes*, Toronto: McGraw-Hill Ryerson.

Wildasin, David E. (1997), 'Fiscal Aspects of Evolving Federations: Issues for Policy and Research', in David E. Wildasin (ed.), *Fiscal Aspects of Evolving Federations*, New York: Cambridge University Press, pp. 14–37.

Wilson, Richard W. (2000), 'The many voices of political culture: assessing different approaches', *World Politics*, 52: 246–73.

Wincott, Daniel (1996), 'Federalism and the European Union: the scope and limits of the Treaty of Maastricht', *International Political Science Review*, 17: 403–15.

World Trade Organization (2001), *International Trade Statistics 2001*, http://www.wto.org/english/res_e/statis_e/its2001_/its01_toc_e.htm (accessed on 15 March 2002).

Zeigler, L. Harmon (1988), *Pluralism, Corporatism, and Confucianism: Political Association and Conflict Regulation in the United States, Europe, and Taiwan*, Philadelphia: Temple University Press.

Ziltener, Patrick (2000a), 'EC Regional Policy: Monetary Lubricant of Regional Integration?', in Volker Bornschier (ed.), *State-building in Europe: The Revitalization of Western European Integration*, Cambridge: Cambridge University Press, pp. 122–51.

——— (2000b), 'EC Social Policy: The Defeat of the Delorist Project', in Volker Bornschier (ed.), *State-building in Europe: The Revitalization of Western European Integration*, Cambridge: Cambridge University Press, pp. 152–83.

Index

Notes: Italic page numbers refer to tables & figures; numbers in brackets preceded by *n* are note numbers.